Reference Training in Academic Libraries

CLIP Note #24

D1535902

Compiled by

Kimberley Robles
Reference & Multicultural Librarian
California State University, Fresno
Fresno, California

Neal Wyatt
Research Consultant, Rare Book Collection
Agecroft Hall
Richmond, Virginia

College Library Information Packet Committee
College Libraries Section
Association of College and Research Libraries
A Division of the American Library Association
Chicago 1996

The paper used in this publication meets the minimum requirements of American National Standard for Information Sciences–Permanence of Paper for Printed Library Materials, ANSI Z39.48-1992. ∞

Library of Congress Cataloging-in-Publication Data
Reference training in academic libraries / compiled by Kimberley
    Robles, Neal Wyatt.
            p.   cm. -- (CLIP note ; #24)
        Includes bibliographical references
        ISBN 0-8389-7842-8 (alk. paper)
        1. Academic libraries--Reference services. 2. Library education
(Continuing education) 3. Reference librarians--Training of.
I. Robles, Kimberley. II. Wyatt, Neal. III. Association of College
and Research Libraries. College Library Information Packet
Committee. IV. Series: CLIP notes ; #24.
Z675.U5R443   1996
023'.8--dc20   96-20726

Printed in the United States of America.

00 99 98 97 96   5 4 3 2 1

Table of Contents

STRUCTURE OF TRAINING

Arizona State University West
Fletcher Library
Phoenix, Arizona

Columbus College
Simon Schwob Memorial Library
Columbus, Georgia

Oberlin College
Oberlin College Library
Oberlin, Ohio

Wellesley College
Clapp Library
Wellesley, Massachusetts

REFERENCE DESK / PATRON SERVICE

Le Moyne College
Le Moyne College Library
Syracuse, New York

Ohio Wesleyan University
L.A. Beeghly Library
Delaware, Ohio

Plattsburgh State College – State University of New York
Feinberg Library
Plattsburgh, New York

LIBRARY INSTRUCTION

LIAISON / OUTREACH SERVICES

EVALUATION OF TRAINEE

Tarleton State University
Dick Smith Library
Stephenville, Texas

COMPREHENSIVE TRAINING DOCUMENTS

Hope College
Van Wylen Library
Holland, Michigan

Marymount University
Reinsch Library
Arlington, Virginia

University of Richmond
Boatwright Library
Richmond, Virginia

William Paterson College
Askew Library
Wayne, New Jersey

CLIP Note Committee

Elizabeth A. Sudduth, Chair
McGraw-Page Library
Randolph-Macon College
Ashland, Virginia

Roxann Bustos
Reese Library
Augusta College
Augusta, Georgia

Doralyn H. Edwards
Richard J. Daley Library
University of Illinois, Chicago
Chicago, Illinois

Carol Goodson
Ingram Library
West Georgia College
Carrollton, Georgia

Jamie A. Hastreiter
William Luther Cobb Library
Eckerd College
St. Petersburg, Florida

Lawrie Merz
Willard J. Houghton Library
Houghton College
Houghton, New York

Lewis Miller
Irwin Library
Butler University
Indianapolis, Indiana

Introduction

Objective

The *College Library Information Packet* (*CLIP*) *Note* publishing program, under the auspices of the College and Research Libraries Section of the Association of College and Research Libraries, provides "college and small university libraries with state-of-the-art reviews and current documentation on library practices and procedures of relevance to them" (Morein 1985). This *CLIP Note* provides information on and ideas for the training of new reference librarians in small and medium-sized academic libraries.

Background

Reference librarians are increasingly being called upon to play a multitude of roles. No longer are basic desk reference and online searching the parameters of the job. Currently, web pages, networked campuses, community outreach, and distance education are all falling under the purview of today's reference librarians. The reference environment is not only changing rapidly, but many new librarians are entering the field as reference librarians. As Reser and Schuneman have pointed out, academic reference positions have accounted for roughly forty-nine percent of the total academic library positions advertised (Reser, Schuneman 1992). The number of reference librarians starting in a new position each year constitutes a significant portion of the work force in the profession. With these developments in mind, it is clear that good training is an essential component of any reference department.

The importance of good training cannot be over emphasized. The training new reference librarians receive is their first introduction to the library and new colleagues, and many people believe that how it is done can be in great part a predictor of that librarian's future success and attitude toward the department and the library. It is also the foundation upon which the new librarian will understand and support the library's mission and service. Training equips librarians with the necessary skills to be a success in the library. It enables them to become oriented to their new surroundings quickly and comfortably; be at ease in their new environment and with their new colleagues; adapt to their new duties; and reach a level of competency with the unfamiliar tools and procedures of the new library. Most importantly, it also enables the new librarian to provide the highest levels of assistance to those who ask for help. Top-notch training allows the skills of the librarian to be quickly put to use in the new library environment and creates an atmosphere where knowledge and further learning are encouraged and enhanced. In other words, good training allows good librarians to excel rather than sink in an overload of new information.

Reference training can vary by many factors, such as the experience level of the newly hired librarian, the position being filled, or the mission of the particular library or institution. Training can consist of a simple check list or an elaborate system with reviews and progress reports. Whatever the format, training by its very nature exists on a continuum, from the first day of orientation to learning a new skill years later. Regardless of their scope or duration, all programs that are effective can be useful in planning a new, or revising an existing training program. Excellent training and policies can be emulated if examples are available.

This *CLIP Note*, by exploring the implementation of training programs in small and medium sized academic libraries, provides data on a variety of programs worthy of emulation. Taking the broadest view possible of training, we studied how these libraries were responding to the changing demands on the profession. We considered training documentation for both new librarians (defined as recent library school graduates) and experienced librarians who have joined a particular reference department that is new to them. The *CLIP Note* focuses on the following areas of reference training: desk service, reference collection and subject specialist knowledge, database training, Internet services, technical training, library instruction, outreach responsibilities and skills, and evaluation of both the trainee and the program.

Survey Procedure

The procedure followed was the standard one for *CLIP Note* projects. The *CLIP Note* Committee of ACRL's College Libraries Section approved a proposal and reviewed drafts of a questionnaire. In August 1995, 265 small and medium-sized academic libraries received the revised questionnaire. The *CLIP Note* mailing list consisted of libraries classified by the Carnegie Foundation for the Advancement of Teaching, as either Comprehensive University and College I or Liberal Arts Colleges I, in their *Classification of Institutions of Higher Learning* (1994). All libraries had previously agreed to participate in *CLIP Note* surveys. In addition to completing the questionnaire, some libraries provided copies of their reference training documents. A selection of these documents, along with the tabulated questionnaire, and complete summaries of the responses comprises this *CLIP Note*.

REFERENCE TRAINING IN ACADEMIC LIBRARIES SURVEY

Thank you for taking the time to answer this survey!

Please circle the appropriate letter to answer each question.
If specific information is requested, please write in the blank space provided.

*The survey itself takes approximately **20 minutes** to complete.*

Institution and Library Profile

Institution Name: _____

Library Name: _____

Address: _____

_____

Name of Respondent: _____

Title: __**Director: 113**_____**Reference: 48**_____**Public Services: 20**_____**Other: 25**__

Email address: _____

Business Telephone: (   ) _____   Fax: (   ) _____

ALL FIGURES REQUESTED ARE FOR FALL 1995 OR FISCAL YEAR 1994-95

1. Public institution   *51 (25%)*   Private institution   *154 (75%)*

2. Number of full-time equivalent (FTE) students enrolled   *2587 (mean)   193 respondents*

3. Number of FTE librarians   *7 (mean) 204 respondents*

4. Number of FTE reference librarians   *3 (mean) 196 respondents*

5. Size of reference collection (# of titles)   *8811 (mean) 161 respondents*

•TRAINING DESIGN•

6. Does your library have a training program for newly hired reference librarians?
    203 respondents

86	a. yes	42%
117	b. no	58%

7. Do you have a written policy or statement of goals for your library's training program?
    89 respondents

7	a. yes	8%
82	b. no	92%

8. What does your reference training program cover? **(circle all that apply)**
    88 respondents

85	a. the reference collection	96%
88	b. electronic resources	100%
85	c. reference desk procedures	96%
83	d. reference service policies	94%
76	e. telephone reference policies	86%
68	f. tours of other library departments	77%
28	g. other (please describe in space provided)	32%

    other nearby library collections; cross training in other departments; related campus offices; campus orientation; special collections; emergency procedures

9. Do you have a checklist of expected competencies for **any** part of your reference training?
    88 respondents

11	a. yes	12%
77	b. no	88%

10. What resources did you use to determine/compile the list(s) of expected competencies?
    (e.g. published works, department meetings, etc.)
    11 respondents

    *small work group; past experience; job descriptions;
    professional and departmental meetings*

11. How do you determine a newly hired librarian's knowledge of sources? **(circle all that apply)**
    86 respondents

41	a. assessment interview	48%
0	b. written pretest	
19	c. other method(s) (please describe)	22%

    *annual evaluation process; informal feedback from colleagues; observation at
    reference desk; determined during search process; double schedule until competent*

36	d. our library does not pretest	42%

12. Are there different individuals responsible for coordinating (scheduling, overseeing, etc.), and
    creating/reviewing/updating the training program?
    84 respondents

11	a. yes (please identify by title)	13%
73	b. no (the same individual or department does both)	87%

•STRUCTURE OF TRAINING•

13. How is your training schedule arranged? **(circle only one)**
    89 respondents
18	a. general schedule followed by all newly hired reference librarians	*20%*
26	b. different schedules/tracks based on librarian's previous experience	*29%*
45	c. we do not have a set training schedule	*51%*

14. What is the duration of your training program? **(circle only one)**
    88 respondents
28	a. 15 or fewer hours	*32%*
19	b. 16 to 39 hours	*22%*
7	c. 40 to 79 hours	*8%*
1	d. 80 hours or more	*1%*
28	e. continuing programs	*32%*
5	f. other	*6%*

    as long as it takes; semester long; ongoing monitoring

15. Do you use any of the following tools when training newly hired librarians? **(circle all that apply and identify the type of training the tool covers)**
    89 respondents
6	a. videos	*7%*
4	b. audiotapes	*4%*
2	c. presentation software (PowerPoint, etc.)	*2%*
54	d. manuals	*61%*
12	e. diagrams, flowcharts, etc.	*13%*
3	f. interactive CAI (Computer Assisted Instruction) CD-ROMs, expert systems, etc.	*3%*
11	g. passive CAI (view only, does not require input from the person being trained) CD-ROMS, tutorials, etc.	*12%*
20	h. other (please describe in the space provided)	*22%*

    audio tour; slide/tape program; meetings notebook for past year to present; newsletter; assigned mentor; past 2 annual reports (department and library)

29	i. none of the above	*33%*

16. Do newly hired librarians have an opportunity to structure any part of their own training?
    88 respondents
61	a. yes (please describe in the space provided)	*69%*

    visits to other departments; practice time on tools; can identify areas in which they want special or additional help; informal training after scheduled training completed; they are given orientation and manuals and plan their own schedule for learning specific responsibilities; newly hired librarians work with Library Director & Reference Services Librarian to determine length of training period

27	b. no	*31%*

17. When assigning training responsibilities, does your library use individuals **other than or in addition to** reference staff for any of the following areas? (choose all that apply and identify by position)

  83 respondents

  33 a. desk/patron services   *40%*

  ILL; Circulation; Media; Reader's Services Librarian; staff in other public service departments; periodicals, government documents; public services librarian

  7 b. the reference collection   *8%*

  periodicals, government documents; Library Director

  16 c. faculty liaison or outreach to student groups   *19%*

  Asst. Dean for Public Services; Head of Collection Development; Library Director; Asst. Director

  42 d. no (all trainers for these areas are from the reference department)   *51%*

•DESK/PATRON SERVICE•

18. How do you teach newly hired librarians about the levels of service offered and types of questions asked at your reference desk? **(circle all that apply)**

  88 respondents

  80   a. by observation (new librarian observes co-worker at desk)   *91%*
  44   b. by shadowing (experienced librarian follows new hire)   *50%*
  72   c. by situation (as a question arises while new librarian works the desk alone)   *82%*
  53   d. provide copies of written policies   *60%*
  24   e. provide sample reference questions   *27%*
  1   f. no training provided   *1%*
  11   g. other (please describe in the space provided)   *13%*

  CA State Core Training program; new librarian always works as a double; dialogue between Reference Coordinator & new hire about the institution's reference service philosophy; oral review; discussions and reference meetings

19. Do you provide training/explain policies for different levels of service to various patron categories (faculty, students, administrators, non-affiliated users, etc.)?

  84 respondents

  35   a. yes (please describe and enclose copies of training)   *42%*

  described in reference policies & procedures manual; verbal explanation

  10   b. no training provided   *12%*
  39   c. no difference in services provided to various patrons   *46%*

20. Does your library provide reference services through any of the following? **(circle all that apply)**

  87 respondents

  87   a. telephone   *100%*
  57   b. regular mail   *66%*
  64   c. email   *74%*
  43   d. fax   *49%*
  12   e. library Web page   *14%*
  6   f. gopher   *7%*
  0   g. none of the above   *0%*

21. Do you have separate training polices and/or procedures for reference services provided via any of the options from question #20?

     88 respondents
      13   a. yes   15%
      75   b. no   85%

22. Are newly hired librarians specifically trained in your library's mission, goals, and ethical standards?

     87 respondents
      71   a. yes   82%
      16   b. no   18%

23. Does your training include the "reference interview" or other communication skills?

     87 respondents
      62   a. yes   71%
      25   b. no   29%

24. Does your training cover communication or awareness issues for interaction with diverse patron groups?

     88 respondents
      37   a. yes   42%
      51   b. no   58%

25. Does your training cover dealing with difficult patrons or situations?

     87 respondents
      61   a. yes   70%
      26   b. no   30%

•REFERENCE COLLECTION•

26. What methods are used to familiarize newly hired librarians with your Reference Collection?

     89 respondents
      85   a. encourage them to browse the collection on their own   96%
      43   b. review specific subject areas with subject experts   48%
      24   c. other (please describe in the space provided)   27%

receive a list of major reference sources; highlight various highly used sources in walking tour of collection; have new librarian assist in inventory of the references collection; assigned to develop a specific section; completing sample questions using specific reference sources; assigned to shelf read; talk about typical questions; encourage the shelving of reference books for familiarization purposes; work on bibliographic aides for specific subject areas

27. Do you use any of the following tools to help newly hired librarians learn your reference collectio
(circle all that apply)
   76 respondents

13	a. reference shelf list	17%
17	b. published bibliographies	22%
50	c. locally created bibliographies	66%
31	d. sample reference questions	41%
0	e. expert systems	0%
2	f. hypertext resources	3%
1	g. CAI (Computer Assisted Instruction)	2%
53	h. online catalog	70%
5	i. other (please describe in the space provided)	7%

   *guided tours; new reference books are kept separate for 1-2 weeks
   for staff review; class handouts*

•DATABASE TRAINING•

28. Who trains newly hired librarians for online search services? (DIALOG, STN, etc.)
   87 respondents

62	a. reference librarians	71%
34	b. vendor workshops	39%
11	c. systems librarian	13%
9	d. instruction librarian	10%
3	e. library does not offer mediated search services	3%
9	f. other	10%

   *we expect them to have this skill when hired; we do very little
   online searching these days—no need to train; only certain reference librarians do online searching—very few done; everyone*

29. Who trains newly hired librarians on the use of end user databases?(CD-ROMs, catalog, etc.)
   89 respondents

82	a. reference librarians	92%
14	b. vendor workshops	16%
11	c. systems librarian	12%
10	d. instruction librarian	11%
0	e. library does not have end user databases	0%
9	f. other	10%

   *any other librarian; paraprofessional information providers;
   everyone; Library Director; reference assistants*

30. Is training provided for any specific end user database or software interface? (e.g. Wilson, SilverPlatter)
   88 respondents

75	a. yes	85%
13	b. no	15%

31. How is the training for end user databases accomplished? **(circle all that apply)**
    88 respondents

84	a. one-on-one session(s) with trainer	*95%*
52	b. manuals/directions for librarians to learn at their own pace	*59%*
27	c. tutorial programs	*31%*
6	d. other (please describe in the space provided)	*7%*

    BI classes; free time to familiarize self and ask specific questions; in-house seminars

32. Who trains newly hired librarians on the use of electronic sources available only at the reference desk? (i.e. bibliographic databases such as OCLC, electronic ready-reference resources, etc.)
    89 respondents

28	a. head of reference	*31%*
54	b. reference librarian(s)	*61%*
9	c. systems librarian	*10%*
6	d. other	*7%*

    paraprofessional information providers; a FAQ book; Library Director

17	e. no electronic resources available only at the reference desk	*20%*

•INTERNET SERVICES•

33. Does your library have access to the Internet?
    89 respondents

87	a. yes	*98%*
2	b. no	*2%*

34. Access to the Internet is available to:
    87 respondents

18	a. staff only (at non-public stations)	*21%*
69	b. both staff and patrons	*79%*

35. Who provides Internet training for newly hired librarians? **(circle all that apply)**
    86 respondents

67	a. reference dept.	*78%*
23	b. systems librarian	*27%*
28	c. campus computer services	*33%*
4	d. no training provided (if no, proceed to question #37)	*5%*
11	e. other(s) (please specify job title(s) in the space provided)	*13%*

    experienced librarians, workshops, Internet tutorials like RoadMap;
    Electronic Librarian; Internet Resources Committee; Instruction
    Librarian; Capcon Workshops

36. How is the Internet training accomplished? **(circle all that apply)**
    83 respondents

75	a. one-on-one session(s) with trainer	*90%*
54	b. workshop(s)	*65%*
38	c. manuals/directions for librarians to learn at their own pace	*46%*
10	d. sample exercises for librarians to complete on their own	*12%*
5	e. other (please describe in the space provided)	*6%*

> *experienced librarians, workshops, Internet tutorials like RoadMap; one-on-one training is arranged upon request; currently under development; discussion*

•TECHNICAL TRAINING•

37. Who provides training to your newly hired librarians on desktop computers? (file management, software programs, etc.)
    89 respondents

35	a. reference librarians	*39%*
29	b. systems librarian	*33%*
42	c. campus computer services	*47%*
6	d. no desktop computer provided/available	*7%*
16	e. no training provided	*18%*
14	f. other	*16%*

> *secretaries; tutorial, manuals; library assistants; librarians; Library Automation Department; colleagues; Electronic Reference Librarian; campus computer services; reference clerk*

38. Who provides training on the technical aspects of computers at the reference desk or in the reference area? (i.e. disk formatting, printer problems, downloading, etc.)
    89 respondents

60	a. reference librarians	*67%*
32	b. systems librarian	*36%*
11	c. no training provided	*12%*
20	d. other	*22%*

> *anyone who knows; paraprofessional staff; campus computer center personnel; reference library assistant; Electronic Reference Librarian; reference clerk*

•LIBRARY INSTRUCTION•

39. Does your library offer library instruction?
    89 respondents

89	a. yes	*100%*
0	b. no	*0%*

40. Are your reference librarians responsible for library instruction?
    89 respondents

86	a. yes	*97%*
3	b. no	*3%*

41. Who provides library instruction training to newly hired reference librarians?
   (circle all that apply)
   87 respondents

49	a. reference librarians	*56%*
38	b. the library instruction coordinator	*44%*
17	c. no formal training, but can observe class sessions of others	*20%*
3	d. no training provided for library instruction	*3%*
23	e. other (please specify trainer's job title in the space provided)	*26%*

   team teach with new librarian; can observe class sessions of others; new librarian observed by experienced librarian; coordinator reviews lesson plans, etc. as needed; Library Director; assigned to help Library Instruction Coordinator

•LIAISON/OUTREACH•

42. Do your reference librarians have responsibilities as faculty liaisons or for outreach to student groups?
   88 respondents

71	a. yes	*81%*
17	b. no	*19%*

43. Is training provided for liaison or outreach activities?
   73 respondents

35	a. yes (please describe in space provided)	*48%*

   Collection Development Head reviews policies, procedures; review of program elements and review of initial activities; one-on-one, group sessions, and written policies/procedures; Library Director conducts workshop; responsibilities are explained, introductions made; periodic workshops and regular meetings; covered in reference manual; basic & general but includes name of department chair, budgeted amount for department and awareness of budget dates

38	b. no	*52%*

•EVALUATION OF TRAINEE•

44. Does your library training program include follow up procedures to measure the effectiveness of the training?
   87 respondents

26	a. yes	*30%*
61	b. no	*70%*

45. Does your training program include additional or advanced training after the newly hired librarian has been in place for a while?
   88 respondents

47	a. yes	*53%*
41	b. no	*47%*

46. How often is the training revised and updated? **(circle only one)**
    80 respondents

15	a. yearly	*19%*
7	b. every five years	*9%*
58	c. other (please specify in the space provided)	*72%*

    we all share information both formally at meetings, informally, and via e-mail; whenever we have a new hire; after each new hire is trained; in response to changes in services; reviewed before new person starts if time permits; reference checklist is updated about every other year

47. Does the trainee have an opportunity to provide formal or informal feedback on the training program?
    88 respondents

82	a. yes	*93%*
6	b. no	*7%*

48. Overall, how would you rate the training in your library for newly hired reference librarians?
    85 respondents

5	a. outstanding	*6%*
26	b. very good	*30%*
50	c. satisfactory	*59%*
4	d. poor	*5%*

49. Do you think your training for newly hired reference librarians needs improvement?
    87 respondents

73	a. yes	*84%*
14	b. no	*16%*

May we publish your documents in a *CLIP Notes* publication?

___I give permission to publish in a *CLIP Note* the documents submitted with this completed survey.
___Permission to publish in a *CLIP Note* the documents submitted with this survey requires the following copyright statement:

•Thank you for filling out this survey•

Please enclose  *sample documents*

Analysis of Survey Results

General Information *(Questions 1-5)*

A total of 206 of the 264 questionnaires were returned for a 78% response rate. Private institutions accounted for three fourths (75%) of the responses while public institutions accounted for one fourth (25%) of the responses. The respondents as a whole reported an average of three FTE reference librarians and an average reference collection of approximately 8811 titles. Overall, the libraries with larger student bodies and higher numbers of full time librarians tended to have training programs in place. Those libraries that did not have training tended to have fewer reference librarians, averaging two per department.

An important factor to note is that out of the 206 respondents, a majority (57%) indicated that they did not have a training program for newly hired reference librarians. Many noted that their libraries were either too small or that turnover occurred so infrequently that any written training documents would be outdated before a need for them arose. The remaining 43% (89 respondents) completed the entire survey, answering questions 7-49. It should also be noted that respondents often checked more than one answer to each question, resulting in a larger pool of responses than respondents. All percentages are based on the total number of responses per question rather than the total number of respondents to the questionnaire itself. For clarity both the total number of respondents and the total number of responses have been provided. Some respondents skipped questions and therefore the total number of respondents does not always equal 89. Contradictory responses (selecting both "yes" and "no" for example) were deemed invalid and not counted. Finally, many of the questions provided space for more expansive answers. In several cases (questions 28, 35, and 41), respondents used this space to expand upon or broaden their responses. We felt it was very important to include these responses because they reflect the current concerns and interests of the participating libraries.

While it was no surprise that Library Directors and Reference Department Heads were the most likely people to complete this survey, there were more than twenty additional job titles listed including Administrative Assistant, Reader Services Librarian, Team Leader, Chairperson, and Librarian.

Training Design *(Questions 6-12)*

Only seven libraries (8%) reported having a written policy or statement of goals for their training programs. This *CLIP Note* provides examples of these policies that can serve as a foundation or a starting point for other libraries that are revising or initiating training programs. That such a large percentage (92%) of all responding libraries did not have written goals is somewhat surprising. Determining or organizing what the library hopes to accomplish would seem to be both an initial and an essential aspect of establishing a training program or of any other endeavor.

Only 12% of the responding libraries had a checklist of expected competencies for any aspect of assumed knowledge. This could indicate a number of possibilities: that most training is assumed to be comprehensive; that library school programs are effective in teaching basic competencies; or that the interview process provides an avenue to determine expected competencies. However, 62% used some kind of method, be it an interview, informal discussion, or observation by experienced colleagues to determine the newly hired librarian's level of knowledge.

Structure of Training *(Questions 13-17)*

The majority of libraries (51%) had no set training schedule, but the length of most training programs was less than two weeks. The two responses that were chosen most frequently (for a combined 54%) were training programs that lasted two days or less (32%) and those lasting not more than a week (22%). Only 1% of libraries trained for two weeks or more, but a higher percentage (28%) had some type of continuing program in place.

The tools most often used for training were manuals, but a combined 16% used some newer technologies in training (presentation software and computer assisted instruction). Many libraries (69%) permitted the newly hired librarian to have some type of input (formal or informal) in the training schedule.

While most trainers were from the Reference Department (51%), a little less than half (40%) of the libraries used staff from the Circulation and Inter-Library Loan Departments to provide some of the desk/patron services training. Some of the liaison/outreach training was conducted by collection development librarians, but it is interesting to note that many libraries reported their directors handled this training.

Training Areas

Desk and Patron Service *(Questions 18-25)*

As expected, many of the respondent libraries used a combination of training methods when teaching the levels of service offered at the reference desk as well as when covering the types of questions most frequently asked. Most libraries used a mix of trainer/trainee methods: observation while working with the new librarian at the reference desk (91%), shadowing the trainee as they take primary responsibility for coverage of the desk (50%), and providing written policies (60%). However, a large majority (82%) of all respondent libraries chose a situational training method that placed the new librarian alone at the reference desk until a problem arose.

Close to half (42%) of the respondents explained their differing service levels for various patron groups either verbally or through policy and procedure manuals. A similar percentage (46%) reported that there was no difference in services between patron categories, indicating that the "equitable service policies" of the ALA *Code of Ethics* (1996) holds sway. The small difference in these two statistics (42% and 46%), may reflect the complexity of the non-affiliated patron issue. Eugene Mitchell (1995) provides a detailed analysis of this topic in *CLIP Note* 21.

All respondent libraries (100%) provided phone assistance and more than half (66%) answered reference queries through regular mail. Almost half (49%) provided reference service via fax. Reflecting the rapidly changing nature of reference services, a large majority (74%) of the respondents indicated that they provided reference via email, many (14%) did so via a Web page, and a few (7%), provided reference assistance via a gopher menu. Despite the growing technological base of reference service and the differing demands and skills required for optimum use of these media, almost all (85%) of the libraries responding reported that there were no separate training procedures in place for these new mediums. Considering the problems these technologies can create (returned/user unknown email, systems that go down, and URLs that change addresses), it seems that the technology has grown so fast that libraries are just keeping up with applications and have not yet found time to implement training programs on, or develop policies for use.

Most respondents provided training or explanations of their libraries' goals, missions, and ethical standards (82%), communication skills (71%), and dealing with difficult patrons (70%). Less than half (42%) provided training for diversity issues, but some mentioned meetings, discussions, and workshops where the topic was raised. Others noted that this type of information was included in their general reference or policy manuals.

Reference Collection *(Questions 26 and 27)*

The most popular method for new librarians to familiarize themselves with the reference collection was to browse alone (96%), but it was encouraging to see that, in addition to this method, many libraries (48%) used specific subject experts or experienced colleagues to provide tours and interpretation of the collection.

The library's catalog and local bibliographies were the tools most frequently used in assisting this training (70% and 66% respectively). A significant percentage (41%) used sample reference questions and a representative number (17%) used the reference shelf list. No one in the survey used expert systems, although two reporting using hypertext documents.

Database Training *(Questions 28-32)*

Reference librarians did most of the online searching training (71%), but over a third (39%) also made use of vendor workshops. A much smaller percentage (12% and 11% respectively), had either the system librarian or the instruction librarian provide training. Three libraries indicated they do not offer mediated searching at all and several others indicated that doing so was rare.

The use of end-user databases, however, was universal among the surveyed libraries, with no library indicating they were not available. Reference librarians provided nearly all (92%) of the training, but vendor workshops were used occasionally (16%). While most (85%) libraries provided training on specific databases and nearly all (95%) offered that training through one-on-one sessions with the trainer, over half (59%) used manuals, and close to a third (31%) used tutorial programs to allow the new librarians to learn at their own pace. A surprising 20% did not have electronic resources (such as OCLC) available only for librarians at the reference desk.

Internet Services *(Questions 33-36)*

Reflecting the progressive nature of most libraries, nearly all (98%) of the respondents indicated that their library had access to the Internet and the majority (79%) of respondents had this access available to both patrons and staff. The statistics here match the indications of the previous section with reference librarians providing most (78%) of the training in one-on-one sessions (90%). This seems to suggest that most reference librarians are expected to be competent enough to train others rather than only to be skilled enough to use the Internet. Reflecting the growing trend for holistic campuses, one third (33%) of libraries make use of the services of campus computer departments to help in their training.

Technical Training *(Questions 37 and 38)*

Technical training is the one area that seems to be rather evenly divided between the Reference (39%), Systems (33%), and Campus Computer Services (47%) Departments — often involving some combination of the three. Training for the technical operations at or around the reference desk (downloading, etc.) however, was provided almost exclusively (67%) by reference librarians. There was still a sizeable group (18%) that did not provide any technical training at all. One possible interpretation is that some technical skills are needed, but the training has yet to catch up with the changing roles of the reference librarian. It also reflects the "who's doing what" question which is discussed in current library literature.

Library Instruction *(Questions 39-41)*

All (100%) of the respondents indicated that they offer library instruction, and nearly all (97%) of the libraries provide training in this area. Reference librarians do the majority (56%) of this training, although a significant number of libraries (44%) have a library instruction coordinator who assists in the training as well. A very small percentage (3%) offer no training whatsoever.

Observation either by, or of, the newly hired librarian was the most common training method listed, and in some cases the only method used (20%), which may explain why very few training documents were submitted in this area. However, in light of the importance of library instruction (100% of respondents indicating that they provide such instruction), the *CLIP Note* includes several specific training resources for library instruction in the bibliography in addition to the training documents included in the sample documents section. Although beyond the scope of the *CLIP Note*, this important service in academic libraries warrants further research. A more focused study may be needed to examine whether adequate training is being provided in light of the shifting paradigms evident in the current library literature.

Liaison and Outreach *(Questions 42 and 43)*

This seems to be an ambivalent area in training programs. While most (81%) of the responding libraries required their reference librarians to undertake liaison responsibilities, a slim majority (52%) did not provide any training in this area.

It seems unrealistic that newly hired librarians, especially those just out of library school, or those from non-academic environments, would have much experience in this type of activity, as it involves not only good political and communication skills but also a high level of understanding of the specific library's general collection and the school's course offerings. In addition, each institution would have differing procedures for accomplishing the various duties liaisons have (communication with the academic departments, ordering and/or tracking requested materials, assessing current holdings in a particular subject area, or the services provided to a department, etc.).

Evaluation

Evaluation of Trainee *(Questions 44 and 45)*

While most libraries (70%) did not have any follow-up procedures to measure the effectiveness of their training programs, more than half (53%) indicated that they do have additional training. Many commented that continuing education was expected at their institutions.

Evaluation of Training Program *(Questions 46-49)*

Most libraries (72%) noted that they updated their training programs when new people were hired, and almost all of them (93%) allowed for feedback from their trainees regarding the training. While over half of the libraries (59%), rated their training as "satisfactory," almost all (84%) felt their training could use some improvement.

Libraries Without Training

In general, questions about the effectiveness of new librarians in a library that chooses not to offer training are unanswered. Most of the respondents included notes or letters listing low turnover rates as the reason they did not offer training. A few others noted that training is an area their libraries need to update or improve. Whatever the reason, the compilers hope this *CLIP Note* will provide sufficient examples to show that training does not necessitate elaborate and formal programs as the only option. Often it is the action of organizing or putting the training on paper that helps librarians think about their libraries from the point of view of the newly hired librarian. *What does he or she need to know about working in this library? What are the unique aspects of our library and/or its services? What are the "expectations" for librarians when providing reference service or library instruction in our library? What are our mission and goals? What are our ethical standards?* These are the kinds of questions good training can address to make newly hired librarians confident and an integral part of their new library setting.

Conclusion

The training of newly hired reference librarians in small and medium sized academic libraries varies from institution to institution but three areas remain common: most training is conducted by reference librarians (from instructional techniques to Internet competence); a combination of methods is used (written documents, guided tours, independent inquiry, observation, one-on-one sessions); and in most cases the newly hired librarians have the opportunity either to participate in the structuring of their training (69%) or provide feedback on the training they received (73%).

The time and effort required to create and implement a training program need not be extensive. Of course, both will take time, but the benefits gained in relation to the energy expended are well worth the effort. Several examples included in this *CLIP Note* are one page in length but reflect clear thinking and cover such vital aspects as organizational structures, services or areas that are emphasized, and acceptable or common approaches and techniques to specific responsibilities.

The training of newly hired reference librarians is vital to both the new librarian and to the institution. Without proper training the investment of both may not be fully realized. Not only does creating a written training document provide the necessary guidance for a new librarian (or for a temporary hire while a permanent worker is on leave) but it, perhaps most importantly, gives the reference department as a whole an opportunity to define its policies, search out and correct its weak points, and reflect upon its mission and the best way to achieve it. In the busy world of reference desks and library instruction schedules, having words written down that remind us of what we do and why we do it is invaluable.

Selection of Documents

The documents that were supplied and are reproduced in this *CLIP Note* illustrate a variety of training methods and philosophies. Documents were selected to illustrate each type of training listed in the survey, with the exception of database training. The majority of documents submitted in this area were designed for the use of patrons rather than the training of librarians. If there were several approaches to the same training, the most unique and easily replicable in other libraries were chosen.

Acknowledgments

We were very fortunate to receive a variety of training documents and would like to thank all the libraries that sent them along with their completed surveys. We would also like to thank those libraries, while not included on the ACRL *CLIP Note* mailing list, who participated in an early Internet version of this survey. Their participation provided the necessary data to proceed with the larger project. We particularly would like to thank Larry Benson at Brigham Young University, Elizabeth Dilworth at Hennepin County Medical Center, Bernice Lacks at California State University, Fresno, Allyson Martin at Dixie College, Diana Shonrock at Iowa State University, Joy Tillotson at Memorial University of Newfoundland, and Trudi Di Trolio at University of Florida. We would also like to express our appreciation to Janet Bancroft. Her assistance in creating the "look" of the questionnaire was invaluable.

Works Cited

American Library Association. *American Library Association Code of Ethics.* Chicago: ALA,
  1996.

Carnegie Foundation for the Advancement of Teaching. *A Classification of Institutions of
  Higher Learning.* Princeton, NJ: Carnegie Foundation, 1994.

Mitchell, Eugene S. *Library Services for Non-Affiliated Patrons. CLIP Note* 21. Chicago: ALA,
  1995.

Morein, P. Grady. "What is a *CLIP Note?" College & Research Library News* 46.5 (1985): 226-
  229.

Reser, David W. and Anita P. Schuneman. "The Academic Library Job Market: A Content
  Analysis Comparing Public and Technical Services." *College & Research Libraries* 53
  (1992): 49-59.

Selected Bibliography

ACRL Instruction Section Task Force. "Guidelines for Instruction Programs in Academic Libraries." *College and Research Libraries News* 56.11 (1995): 767-69.

American Library Association. *Electronic Resources Skills: An Assessment and Development Log for Reference Staff.* RASD Occasional Paper, 17. Chicago: ALA, 1995.

Arthur, Gwen. "Using Video for Reference Staff Training and Development: A Selective Bibliography." *Reference Services Review* 20.4 (1992): 63-9.

Bessler, Joanne M. *Putting Service into Library Staff Training: A Patron-Centered Approach.* LAMA Occasional Paper Series. Chicago: ALA, 1994.

Bibliographic Instruction Section, Association of College and Research Libraries. *Learning To Teach: Workshops on Instruction.* Chicago: American Library Association, 1993.

Blenkinsopp, Heather. "How's the Water? The Training of Reference Librarians." *The Reference Librarian* 38 (1992): 175-81.

Corbin, John. "Competencies for Electronic Information Services." in *The Public-Access Computer Systems Review* 4.6 (1993): 5-22. [Electronic File] Available from listserv@uhupvm1.uh.edu with message: get Corbin PRV4N6 F=Mail. 27 March 1996.

Edwards, Ralph M. *The Role of the Beginning Librarian in University Libraries.* Chicago: American Library Association, 1975.

Frisch, Paul and John J. Small. "Voice Mail at the Reference Desk." *College and Research Libraries News* 55 (1994): 343-45.

Glogowski, Maryruth Phelps. *Academic Libraries and Training.* Foundations in Library and Information Science 29. Greenwich, CT: JAI, 1994.

Grumling Dennis K. and Carolyn A. Sheehy. "Professional Development Program: Training for Success within Academic Librarianship." *College and Research Libraries* 54 (1993): 17-24.

Johnson, W.G. "The Need for a Value-based Reference Policy: John Rawls at the Reference Desk." *Reference Librarian* 47 (1994): 201-11.

Katz, Bill and Anne Clifford, eds. *Reference and Online Services Handbook: Guidelines, Policies, and Procedures for Libraries.* New York: Neal-Schuman, 1982.

Miller, Anna L. *Reference Service Policies in ARL Libraries.* SPEC Kit 203. Chicago: Association of Research Libraries, 1994.

Nofsinger, Mary M. and Angela S.W. Lee. "Beyond Orientation: The Roles of Senior Librarians in Training Entry-Level Reference Colleagues." *College & Research Libraries* 55.2 (1994): 161-70.

Ristow, Ann. "Academic Reference Service Over Electronic Mail." *College and Research Libraries News* 53 (1992): 631-37.

Roberts, Anne F. and Susan G. Blandy. *Library Instruction for Librarians.* Englewood, CO: Libraries Unlimited, 1989.

Rockman, Ilene F. "Coping with Library Incidents: How to Train Staff with Simulations of Events." *College & Research Libraries News* 56 (1995): 456-57.

Rogers, Shelley L. "Orientation for New Library Employees: A Checklist." *Library Administration & Management* 8 (1994): 213-17.

Schiller, Nancy. "Internet Training and Support. Academic Libraries and Computer Centers: Who's Doing What." *Internet Research* 4.2 (1994): 35-47.

Shonrock, Diana and Craig Muldar. "Instruction Librarians: Acquiring the Proficiencies Critical to Their Work." *College and Research Libraries* 54.2 (1993): 137-49.

Stabler, Karen Y. "Introductory Training of Academic Reference Librarians: A Survey." *RQ* 26 (1987): 363-69.

Vandercook, Sharon, et al. *Reference Manual.* Sacramento: CORE, 1989.

Wogaman, Mariol R. "Training Newly Appointed Reference Librarians." *College & Research Libraries News* 53 (1992): 8-9.

Woodard, Beth. "A Selective Guide to Training Literature for the Reference Librarian/Trainer." *Reference Services Review* 17.1 (1989): 41-51.

Yates, Rochelle. *A Librarian's Guide to Telephone Reference Service.* Hamden, CT: Shoe String Press, 1986.

REFERENCE TRAINING DOCUMENTS

TRAINING DESIGN DOCUMENTS

Augusta College
Reese Library
Augusta, Georgia
Orientation Checklist: Reference Librarians

Humboldt State University
Humboldt State University Library
Arcata, California
Training Checklist for New Library Faculty

Oberlin College
Oberlin College Library
Oberlin, Ohio
*Reference Department Organization and Philosophy
(Notes for new reference librarian orientation)*

Tarleton State University
Dick Smith Library
Stephenville, Texas
Department Orientation

Trenton State College
Roscoe C. West Library
Trenton, New Jersey
Procedures for New Librarian Orientation

REESE LIBRARY

Orientation checklist: Reference Librarians

— Slide/tape program
— Policy and procedures manuals
— Reference desk (Tips filebox, in-out basket, notebooks, hanging files)
— Phone, important numbers, answering machine
— Room 111 bulletin board
— Ready Reference shelves
— Reference stacks (also index tables and new book shelves)
— Foreign language bank
— Vertical files
— Special Collections, manuscripts, etc.
— Handouts
— Opening and closing procedures
— Organizer
— Reference schedule (preferences?)
— Serials holdings
— Interlibrary loan

TRAINING CHECKLIST FOR NEW LIBRARY FACULTY

ACQUISITIONS & COLLECTION DEVELOPMENT:

Introduction to Acquisitions/Biblio
Requisitions (equipment; supplies; personal books)
On Order File
Introduction to collection development
Overview of subject specialty assignments
Introduction to faculty in departments related to the subject specialty
    assignments
Serials review
Journals routed for checking/ordering
Baker & Taylor approval process
Choice cards

ADMINISTRATION:

Administrative overview (CSU, HSU, Library)
Collective bargaining/MOU (copy on permanent reserve—see CFA for personal
    copy)
10/12 option
Faculty Handbook
Library Manual
Library Dayfile
Fee waiver (for full-time employees)
Absence reports
Leave forms
Insurance
Payroll (pay periods, automatic deposit, credit union)
Keys
Parking permits

CATALOGING/PERIODICALS:

Introduction to Cataloging/Periodicals/Bindery
Journal routing
Micro readers, copiers, and cabinets
Mail distribution

CIRCULATION/MEDIA:

Introduction to Circulation
Policies for various collections (Reserve, Case, computer software, sound
    recordings, Documents, Humboldt County Collection, Periodicals,
    Current Reading, CLC/Curriculum, pamphlets, maps)
Equipment circulation (headphones, micro readers)
Search/Holds
Shelving
ILL shelf
Introduction to Media Services
Room reservations

DOCUMENTS/HUMBOLDT COUNTY ROOM:

Introduction to Documents/Humboldt County Room

IS DEPARTMENT:

Structure of the department
IS Council and committees
Staff development
IS Policy & Procedures Manual
Goal setting
Vacation and travel plans
REFERENCE SERVICE (see document following)

MISCELLANEA:

Campus orientation
Festivities
Staff room
CFA
Academic Senate
Campus committees

Reference Department Organization & Philosophy
<notes for new reference librarian orientation>

Brief review of orientation & training schedule
    any additional topics? questions?

The Workweek
    number of hours (technically 40)
    typical workweek schedule, compensatory time, lunch hour, breaks
    planned absences (vacation, conferences, etc.)
    unplanned absences (illness, emergency, etc.)
    notifying others of absences & recording dates
        - announce in meetings
        - put on reference desk calendar
        - STF/TIM

The reference desk
    review sample desk schedule during a semester
    evenings & weekends, Fridays off
    swapping desk hours
    fall/spring break, reading period/exams, summer, etc.

Reference department organization
    structure of department & areas of responsibility
    how responsibilities are decided upon
    reference meetings, reference agenda

Reference philosophy
    mission of the library & how reference fits into it
    major clientele & level of service provided
    reference services offered:
        reference desk
        telephone
        by appointment (students & faculty)
        correspondence
        e-mail

Questions??

rev jg 7/95

Tarleton State University

DEPARTMENT ORIENTATION

Check List

This orientation check list is a suggested method for orienting a new employee. It may also be used for a current employee who is transferred or promoted to a new position. By discussing the topics in this check list, the new employee should do a better job, feel welcome to the department, and have a clear understanding of what is expected of him/her. Give a copy of this check list to the employee to follow along as you discuss each item.

Name_____ S.S.#_____ Starting Date_____

Job Title_____ Starting Rate of Pay_____

Department_____ Section_____

Supervisor's Name_____ Telephone Extension_____

A. FUNCTIONS OF SECTION
( ) Function of Department
( ) Function of Section
( ) Organization of Section
( ) Employee Duties and Responsibilities
( ) Performance Standards
( ) Work of Others in Section
( ) Team Work

B. PHYSICAL SURROUNDINGS AND EQUIPMENT
( ) Work Area
( ) Demonstration of Equipment
( ) Location of Supplies
( ) Fire Extinguishers and Exits
( ) Safety Regulations
( ) Work Uniforms
( ) Employee Lounge (Restrooms)
( ) Smoking Area
( ) Parking Facilities
( ) Keys
( ) Bulletin Boards
( ) Name Tags (ID Cards)

C. PAY FOR TIME WORKED
( ) Pay Checks
  ( ) Pay Day
  ( ) Check Pick Up
  ( ) Pay Deductions
  ( ) Pay Complaints (Talk to Supervisor)
  ( ) Rate of Pay
  ( ) Pay Increase (Merit)
  ( ) Overtime Compensation
  ( ) Time Sheets
    ( ) Where to Obtain and Return Sheets
    ( ) How to Complete Sheets

D. PAY FOR TIME NOT WORKED
( ) Holidays
( ) Vacations
  ( ) Eligible for How Many Hours After Six Months
  ( ) When Request Should be Made
  ( ) Completing Form
( ) Sick Leave
  ( ) Eligible for How Many Hours
  ( ) Who and When to Report Absences
  ( ) Completing Form
( ) Emergency Leave
  ( ) Eligible for How Many Days
  ( ) Who and When to Report Absences
  ( ) Completing Form
( ) Jury Leave
  ( ) Who and When to Report Absences
( ) Military Duty
( ) Temporary Disability Leave (Including Maternity)

E. HOURS OF WORK
( ) Define Work Week
( ) Starting Time
( ) Quitting Time
( ) Work Schedule Changes
( ) Required Overtime
( ) Meal Periods
  ( ) When and How Long
( ) Break Periods
  ( ) When and How Long
( ) Medical Appointments

F. RIGHTS AND RESPONSIBILITIES
    ( ) Attendance
    ( ) Punctuality
    ( ) Attitudes
       (Work Rules and Regulations)
    ( ) Conduct and Appearance
    ( ) Corrective Discipline
       ( ) Steps of Discipline and
          Dismissal Policy
    ( ) Complaint and Appeal Procedure
       ( ) Steps of Complaint Procedure
    ( ) Training Opportunities
    ( ) Housekeeping and Sanitation
    ( ) Probation Period
       ( ) Length - 6 months
       ( ) Evaluations - How often, By
          whom, Format
    ( ) Telephone Usage - Including Rules
       about Personal Long Distance Calls
    ( ) Confidential Information
    ( ) Professional Ethics
    ( ) Care of Equipment
    ( ) Leaving During Working Hours
    ( ) Changes in Personal Status
       (Name, Address, etc.)
    ( ) Where to Get Information and Help
    ( ) Job Injuries Reported to Supervisors
    ( ) Disaster - Your Duties

G. MISCELLANEOUS
    ( ) Departmental Bulletin Board
    ( ) Coffee Making Facilities
    ( ) Departmental Parties, Picnics, Etc.
    ( ) Departmental Rules About Class Attendance

Remarks: _____

_____

_____

_____

I have explained to the employee the above topics and have given him/her a copy of this check list.

My supervisor has explained the above topics to me and has given me a copy of this check list.

_____   _____
Supervisor's Signature   Date   Employee's Signature   Date

ROSCOE L. WEST LIBRARY
PROCEDURES FOR NEW LIBRARIAN ORIENTATION

BEFORE NEW LIBRARIAN ARRIVES: (to be accomplished by the staff of the Dean of the Library)

1. Obtain parking tokens and send them to librarian before the first day of work.
2. Assign telephone authorization code.
3. Assign E-mail address.
4. Provide desk supplies.
5. Order library keys.
6. Make appointment for photo ID.
7. Compile packet on housing opportunities and general community information and send to new librarian. (Mercer and Bucks Counties' Chambers of Commerce can supply some of this information.)

DAY ONE OF ORIENTATION: (Arrangements to be made by LFSC)

1. Pick up and sign for library keys.
2. Obtain parking decal and gate key.
3. Tour of the library, with introductions to staff, locations of restrooms, mailboxes, etc,.
4. Schedule someone(s) to take librarian to lunch.
5. Supply packet that includes:
    a) "Official policy file."
    b) Faculty Handbook, when available.
    c) Library Faculty Manual.
    d) New Librarian Orientation.
    e) Librarian goals and objectives.
    f) Campus maps.
    g) Campus directory.
    h) Copy of current Library telephone chain.
    i) Directory of library staff.
    j) Time-off (vacation, sick, leave of absence) forms/policy.
    k) Request for re-imbursement for travel, conferences, and workshops.
    l) Procedures for campus/off campus mail.
    m) Telephone instructions.
    n) Policy on periodical selection.
    o) Calendar and procedure for ordering on campus and off campus supplies.
6. Set up appointment with appropriate staff in Personnel Office.

DAY TWO OF ORIENTATION: (Arrangements to be made by LFSC)

1. Coffee with staff from area in which new librarian will work.
2. New Public Services Librarians should be scheduled for reference desk duty for a part of the day.
3. Meet with Library Faculty Steering Committee for information on the library's committee structure and organizational culture, and to go over information in the Library Faculty Manual.

DAY THREE OF ORIENTATION: (Arrangements to be made by LFSC)
    1. Orientation and coffee with staff from department to which new librarian is not assigned.
    2. Meet with Database Coordinator.

During the course of the orientation, the new librarian should be informed about the following:

    NOTIS, OCLC, On-line services, CD-ROMs/End User Lab, Interlibrary Loan, Curriculum Materials Collection, Rand documents, Music Reference, Materials in Basement (Old Reference, Compact Periodicals, Storage, etc,.), Periodicals, Documents collection, Region C, Reference Room orientation, Science Reference, Children's reference, Special Collection/Archives, Princeton Cards, Reciprocal borrowing information, Classified Continuations file, order cards and procedures, order processing, non-book materials, and the user education program.

STRUCTURE OF TRAINING DOCUMENTS

Arizona State University West
Fletcher Library
Phoenix, Arizona
Library Orientation Schedule

Columbus College
Simon Schwob Memorial Library
Columbus, Georgia
Tentative Schedule – Orientation

Oberlin College
Oberlin College Library
Oberlin, Ohio
Interoffice Memo and Orientation Schedule

Wellesley College
Clapp Library
Wellesley, Massachusetts
Checklist for Orienting Librarians to Reference

Arizona State University West Library
4701 W. Thunderbird Rd.
P.O. Box 37100
Phoenix, Arizona 85069-7100

LIBRARIAN ORIENTATION SCHEDULE

WEEK ONE:

First Week Goals
1) *To understand the organization of the library, know the locations of the different departments, and know the key people in each department.*
2) *To understand the relationship between ASU West and the Tempe campus (including, in general terms, the document delivery system).*
3) *To understand the organization of the campus.*
4) *To understand the organization and functioning of the IRSS department.*
5) *To understand the expectations for the librarians.*
6) *To know how to use the ASU General Catalog and the CARL system.*
7) *To have a basic understanding of the information desk's purpose and function.*
8) *To understand the responsibilities in collection development.*

Monday, July 8

8:00 am   Meet with Carol Hammond, Head of Information and Research Support Services:

          a) Organization of the library and the campus
          b) ASU West relationship with Tempe
          c) Relations with area libraries
          d) Reading list

10:00 am   Building tour with organizational chart and phone list in hand, Dennis Isbell, Research Support Services Librarian:

          a) introductions, (meetings with key people later),
          b) functions of each area (and personnel)-brief descriptions
          c) trainee's office space

11:00 am   Campus tour—general

12:00 pm   Lunch with coworkers

1:30 pm   ASU Online Catalog introduction, Bee Gallegos
          - ASU General Catalog, day one

3:00-5:00 pm Human Resources appointment (scheduled with Judy Reynolds)

5:00 pm   Free time to try Online Catalog, organize desk, etc.

Tuesday, July 9

8:00 am — Meet with Carol Hammond: departmental orientation:

    a) locations, supplies, keys, doors, elevators, vacation requests, sick leave, mail
    b) meetings
    c) communication mechanisms and campus publications

9:00 am — Meet with Hank Harken, Electronic Specialist:

    a) File server
    b) Overview of computer systems in library

11:00 am — ASU Online Catalog, Bee Gallegos—Journal and special indices and practice

LUNCH

2:00 pm — Librarians Caucus Meeting

4:00 pm — Meet with Eleanor Mitchell, Document Delivery Specialist

    a) Explanation of Eleanor's position
    b) Brief introduction to document delivery
    c) Discussion of Library Assistant's training and Edward's place in it

Wednesday, July 10

8:00 am — Tour of Circulation, Reserves and Main Stacks, Sondra Brough

9:00 am — Tour of Computer Access Center, Dennis Richards

10:00 am — Meet with Carol Hammond:

    a) Librarian's responsibilities and relationship to support staff
    b) reading list (see orientation 1/21/91)
    c) brief mention of Evaluation and Review (will be discussed in more detail in third week)

11:00 am — Meet with Marilyn Myers
    - Collection Development responsibilities and procedures

1:30 pm — Telephone Information, Terry Tallent

    a) How to answer
    b) Taking messages
    c) Transferring calls
    d) Hold
    c) Answering machine

3:00 pm — ASU Online Catalog, Bee Gallegos
    CARL and Uncover

Thursday, July 11

| 8:00 am | Discuss Information Desk Manual, Luene Dorsey
- Tour of the desk, Luene Dorsey: |

a) Maps
b) Telephone numbers
c) Desk contents
d) Forms
e) Supplies
f) Document Delivery baskets
g) Periodicals lists, fiche reader
h) Pathfinders

9:00 am   Discussion with LAs—Info Desk Process: Luene, Terry, Sylvia

11:00 am   Tour of Bibliographic Services, Rana Robertson

LUNCH

1:00 pm   Ready Reference Sources, Denise Kolber

3:30 pm   Program Improvement Council Meeting (PIC)

WEEK TWO:

Second Week Goals
1) *To become familiar with the various formats in which periodical indexing can be found, and the process of locating articles in periodicals in-house and beyond.*
2) *To learn the location of collections within the library.*
3) *To become familiar with the reference collection and the reference process.*
4) *To have a basic understanding of the telecommunications system.*
5) *To learn the locations and functions of West Campus departments and become able to direct inquiries functionally and locationally.*
6) *To become familiar with relevant aspects of Tempe campus and understand how the relationship between the libraries is manifested in our resources, tools, and services.*
7) *To become familiar with the resources available at area libraries, and our policies and practices relating to them.*
8) *To understand the faculty liaison function of the librarians.*
9) *To learn the general business sources, both print and CD-ROM.*
10) *To have a basic understanding of the online searching process.*

Monday, July 15

8:00 am   Meet with Anne McKee—Serials

10:00 am   Introduction to Printed Indexes, Dennis Isbell:

   a) Locations, samples
   b) How to read citations
   c) Practice

LUNCH

1:00 pm   CD-ROMS, Lisa Kammerlocher:

   a) Mechanics of system, overview, turning on, etc.
   b) Introduction to one Silverplatter, PsychLit, and sample citations

3:00 pm   Serials and JMM, Eleanor Mitchell:

   a) Serials lists: locate the citations found
   b) Tour of JMM, introduction to processes, holdings, locations
   c) Document Delivery in brief
   d) Reading from Info Desk Manual on Doc Del

Tuesday, July 16

8:00 am   Tour and discussion of locations of collections, Dennis Isbell:

   a) Government Documents
   b) Curriculum
   c) Oversize
   d) Government Serials
   e) Stacks

10:00 am   Tour of reference collection, highlights, Denise Kolber
            - Introduction to types of reference materials

LUNCH

1:00 pm   Discussion of reference and referral process with Librarians and LAs:
            subject areas, kinds of questions, office hours
            - Sample Information Desk Questions, Denise Kolber
            - Readings on Reference Interview
            - Observation at Information Desk

3:30 pm   Meet with Hank Harken—PROFS introduction

Wednesday, July 17

8:00 am   Campus tour with map and directory, Edward Gonzalez

9:30 am   Discussion of directional and campus information, Sylvia Frost
            - Sample questions

10:30 am   Discussion of Tempe and other libraries, Carol Hammond

Arizona State University West • Phoenix, Arizona

11:00 am	Document Delivery, Terry Tallent

2:00 pm	IRSS Department Meeting

3:30 pm   Meet with Carol Hammond:

   a) Faculty liaison (if decided, liaison responsibilities)
   b) Research support
   c) Handbook for faculty

Thursday, July 18

8:00 am   Tour of basic business reference sources, Denise Kolber
   a) Ways of approaching and narrowing a business question
   b) Company information
   c) Industry information
   d) Basic business statistics
   e) Indexes for finding business journal articles
   f) ABI-Inform and BPI on CARL

1:30 pm   Meet with Hank Harken—Telecommunications software

3:00 pm   Meet with Lisa Kammerlocher—Overview of online searching

WEEK THREE:

Third Week Goals
1) To learn the sources for current events and political science, including CD-ROMS
2) To learn the reference sources in Education, including the use of ERIC on CD-ROMS
3) To have a basic understanding of the library's instruction program
4) To understand the continuing appointment and promotion (review) process
5) To learn basic literary and review sources, and sources of book information
6) To have a basic understanding of Campus Governance

Monday, July 22

8:00 am   Tour of basic reference sources for finding information on current
             events, Lisa Kammerlocher
             Learn to use PAIS, Newspaper Abstracts CD-ROMS, and New York
             Times Index as article finding tools

1:00 pm   Tour of basic reference sources in Education, Bee Gallegos
             Learn to use ERIC, Krause Collection, Indexes to Tests, etc.

3:30 pm   Meet with Lisa Kammerlocher, introduction to instruction program

Tuesday, July 23

8:00 am   Tour of literary reference sources, Dennis Isbell

            a) Introduction to sources of film and theater reviews
            b) Introduction to sources of book information (reviews, BIP)

10:00 am   Meet with Carol Hammond and Marilyn Myers, Continuing appointment and promotion:

            a) detailed introduction
            b) three criteria and expectations

2:00-4:00 pm Librarian's Caucus and Collection Development Meeting

Wednesday, July 24

8:00 am   Meet with Marilyn Myers, Campus Governance

ADDITIONAL TRAINING ACTIVITIES TO BE SCHEDULED WHEN AVAILABLE:
       1) PROFS workshop
       2) DIALOG seminar
       3) Tempe libraries tour
       4) Area libraries tours
       5) New faculty and academic professional orientation (Aug. 21, 1991)

DI   6/27/91

Arizona State University West • Phoenix, Arizona

TENTATIVE SCHEDULE

ORIENTATION

TUESDAY, JULY 6.

9:00 - 12:00   GENERAL ORIENTATION

                    Meet with Library Director
                    Human Resources Office
                    Public Safety Office
                        (permit,ID,key)
                    Campus tour
                    Policies(leave, calendar, etc)

11:00 - 12:00   TOUR OF LIBRARY

                    Reference Office Protocols
                    Desktop Computing: LAN
                    Meet Library Faculty and Staff

12:00   LUNCH

1:30 - 5:00   REFERENCE DEPARTMENT ORIENTATION

                    Duties and responsibilities
                    Library philosophy; Teamwork
                    Reference schedule
                        nights and weekends
                    Bibliographic Instruction
             Reference Desk
                    Student Assistants
                    Supplies
                    Questions
                    Library Publications
                      (Reference Notebook,
          Department Policy Manual,
       "Booking Passages" and
    "Library Resources
and Services for Faculty")

5:00 - 6:00   REFERENCE DESK with ERMA

WEDNESDAY, JULY 7

    8:15 - 9:00   BROWSE REFERENCE COLLECTION

    9:00 - 11:00   REFERENCE DEPARTMENT ORIENTATION
                             Continuation........

    11:00 - 12:00   MAR 315 - BI CLASS WITH MERRYLL
                             (Searching UGA and GSU Catalogs)

    12:00 - 1:00   LUNCH

    1:00 - 3:00   Browsing and exploring

    3:00 - 5:00   REFERENCE DESK with SANDRA

THURSDAY, JULY 8

    8:15 - 9:00   BROWSING REFERENCE DEPARTMENT AND
               COLLECTION (U-SEARCH?)

    9:00 - 10:00   INTERLIBRARY LOAN (STAFF)

    10:00 - 11:00   CIRCULATION (STAFF)

    11:00 - 12:00   REFERENCE DESK WITH KIM

    12:00 - 1:00   LUNCH IN CAFETERIA WITH ERMA

    1:00 - 2:00   MEET WITH LIBRARY DIRECTOR

    2:00 - 3:00   GOVERNMENT DOCUMENTS (STAFF)

    3:00 - 5:00   U-SEARCH CD'S

FRIDAY, JULY 9
    8:15 - 10:00   FREE TO BROWSE AND GET READING DONE

    10:00 - 11:00   ARCHIVES WITH CALLIE

    11:00 - 12:00   REFERENCE DESK WITH CALLIE

    12:00 - 1:00   LUNCH

    1:00 - 2:00   FREE TIME

    2:00 - 3:00   ETC: COMPUTERS, COPIERS, AV

    3:00 - 4:00   FIRST FRIDAY

    4:00 - 5:00   REVIEW OF WEEK ONE

WEEK TWO:

CONTINUE REFERENCE & LIBRARY ORIENTATION
VISIT OTHER DEPARTMENTS
LEARN MORE ABOUT COLLEGE

Oberlin College

Oberlin College Library
Interoffice Memo

To: [new reference librarian]
From: [Head of Reference]
Date: October 17, 1995
Re: Orientation

Attached is a *very detailed* (whew!) schedule of training sessions, meetings, and events for the next month or so, designed to orient you to life as a reference librarian here at Oberlin. You'll be introduced to the workings of the Main Library reference department in quite some detail, and also to staff and activities in other units and branches within the library. This may seem an awful lot to absorb during your first weeks here, but it's really meant just to give you an overview of the nuts n' bolts of the way things work around here - so relax and have fun!

Business cards have been ordered for you, and should be arriving soon.

If there is anything that's not covered in your training schedule that you think should be, or if things come up as you go along that you would like a little more training in (like? hm... OCLC? ILL operation? etc.), *please*, just say the word, and we'll set something up.

Last but not least -- we're glad you're here, and look forward to having you as a colleague. Welcome!!

Orientation Schedule, 1995
Oberlin College Library Reference Department
[Name, new reference librarian]

First Week

Tuesday, August 1

9 am   Department of Human Resources (Service Building, 2nd floor)
            If not already accomplished, finalize all employment and
            benefits paperwork, acquire a copy of the A&PS Handbook,
            photo for staff ID card, keys, etc.

10 am   Re-introduction to reference department staff and department
            tour [ref dept member]

**Noon   Lunch with department

1:30 pm   Reference department organization and service philosophy

            [Head of Ref]

            Discuss workweek, reference desk scheduling, breaks, lunch,
            vacation, illness, other absences; mission of the library; structure
            of reference department and areas of responsibility, including
            your specific areas of responsibility; reference meetings and
            agendas.

3-5 pm   Orientation to your office Macintosh [ref dept member]
            What's on it & how to get at it (Word, Netscape, VersaTerm);
            setting up VersaTerm sessions; QuickMail intro (if poss.); access
            to STF through Net-scape; using chooser, printing; accessing CD-
            ROM Network from your Mac.

Wednesday, August 2

11 am   Detailed building tour [Head of Ref]
            Tour of Mudd Center, including staff lounge, receiving room,
            and other non-public areas. Locations of elevators & stairwells,
            and how to get around the building (particularly after hours).

3-5 pm   Reference desk observation
            Begin review of the Reference Desk checklist. Continue working
            through this list during each observation period until
            completed.

Thursday, August 3

10 am   Reference department operations [ref dept member]
            Mail, supplies, student assistants, phones, voicemail, copiers,
            FAX, etc.

3-5 pm   Reference desk observation

Friday, August 4

    10 am   Interlibrary Loan/OCLC overview [ref dept member]
                    General introduction: organization, policies & procedures (charges, etc.); verifying & accepting requests at the reference desk; renewal requests, patron status, NEOMARL

    3-5 pm   Reference desk observation

Second Week

Monday, August 7

    10 am   Government publications overview [ref dept member]
                    General introduction to federal, state, & UN publications; location of collections, shelf list, Marcive, other indexes; how docs are selected & rec'd;arrange for further mtgs. re: gov docs projects at your mutual convenience

    3-5 pm   Reference desk observation

Tuesday, August 8

    9 am   Reference department meeting

    10:30 am   Circulation department [Head of Circulation]

                    Department tour, staff introductions, overview of departmental responsibilities, activities, etc. Barcode for your ID.

    3-5 pm   Reference desk observation

Wednesday, August 9

    9 am   Library Instruction [ref dept member]
                    How we do it here, reminders to faculty, calls, etc.; use of equipment in 202, sign in 102, BI files in department

    11 am   Reference collection development [Head of Ref]
                    How materials are selected for the collections; review of budget; recommending new titles for reference; serials, weeding, barcodes, etc.

    3-5 pm   Reference desk observation

Thursday, August 10

    9 am   Reference Workgroup mtg., Thornton Rm.

    10 am   Business office & stock room tour [Asst. to Director]
                    Staff introductions and overview of activities, services, etc.

    11 am   Meet with Ray English

    3-5 pm   Reference desk observation

Friday, August 11

10 am   Electronic resources in Reference [ref dept members]
Intro. /refreshers as needed: OBIS, Lexis/Nexis, FirstSearch, UnCover, CD-ROM Network, stand-alone CD's, mediated searching (Dialog, VuText, etc.).

1:30 pm   QuickMail [ref dept member]
Basics (if needed): sending, deleting, filing msgs; setting up address books, creating special addresses, updating address books, finding addresses; preferences (changing password, startup options, filing options, mail log, etc.); installing forms; use of the ILL, Reference Query, and Book Order forms

3-5 pm   Reference desk observation

Third Week

Monday, August 14

10 am   Reference Desk Assistants [Head of Ref]
Overview of history, development, purpose, and structure of the RDA program; working at desk with RDA's; what's involved in supervision, evaluation, etc.

3-5 pm   Reference desk observation

5 pm   Photo taken for library newsletter

Tuesday, August 15

10 am   Miscellaneous collections [ref dept member]
ESIC, Women's Studies Reading Room, Asian American Reading Room, flat maps, phone fiche, college catalogs on fiche, etc.

3-5 pm   Reference desk observation

Wednesday, August 16

9:30 am   Library Staff Association [library staff member]
Introduction to the activities and organization of the Library Staff Association; introduction to Staff Association officers

11 am   Collection Development [Head of Collection Development]
Introduction to liaison system and liaison areas. Additional discussions about liaison work should be scheduled at your mutual convenience.

3-5 pm   Reference desk observation

Thursday, August 17

    10 am   Reserve Room [Reserve Rm. supervisor]
                      Tour and overview of reserve activities and policies; how liaison work fits in with the reserve room

    3-5 pm   Reference desk observation

Friday, August 18

    9 am   Monographs Department [Head of Monographs]
                      Department tour, staff introductions, workflow, shelflist, etc.

    1:30 pm   Orientation by Library Forum Orientation Cmtte. [library staff member]
                      Circulation policy for College employees, Library Newsletter, Oberlin Public Library information, etc.

    3-5 pm   Reference desk observation

Fourth Week

Monday, August 21

    3-5 pm   Reference desk observation

Tuesday, August 22

    9 am   Reference department meeting

    3-5 pm   Reference desk observation

Wednesday, August 23

    11 am   Orientation for Library Orientation Tour givers - Thornton Room

    3-5 pm   Reference desk observation

Thursday, August 24

    9 am   Staff convocation - Goodrich Room

    10:30 am   Special Collections/Preservation [Head of Special Collections]
                      Meet in Special Collections, 4th fl., Main Library
                      Department tour, staff introductions, overview of activities, policies, etc. View film on the care and handling of books

    3-5 pm   Reference desk observation

Friday, August 25

    9 am   College Archives [College Archivist]
                      Meet in the Archives, main library, 4th floor
                      Tour, staff introductions, collections strengths, overview of activities, appropriate referrals, etc.

11 am   Conservatory Library [Con. library public services librarian]
        Meet in Conservatory Library in Conservatory Complex. Tour of
        library, staff introductions, collection strengths, overview of
        activities, major reference tools, appropriate referrals, etc.

3-5 pm Reference desk observation

(This will be your last "official" day of desk observation, and you will be scheduled
for regular "solo" desk slots next week; if you would like to do more observation
before going it alone, please just let me know; also, remember that you can call on
any of us at any time for backup!)

Fifth Week

Monday, August 28
        Library orientation tours - all day

Tuesday, August 29
9 am   Audiovisual Department [Head of AV]
        Meet in AV, 4th floor, Main Library
        Department tour, staff introductions, overview of services,
        policies, etc.

10:30 am Serials Department [Head of Serials]
        Department tour, staff introductions, introduction to serials
        acquisitions, check-in, and cataloging workflow. Thornton
        Room collection.

Wednesday, August 30
10 am   Science Libraries & Professional staff evaluations [Science
        Libraian]
        Meet in Science Library, Kettering Hall
        Tour of Science Library and Physics Library (Wright Physics
        Laboratory), staff introductions, collection strengths, overview of
        activities, introduction to major reference tools, appropriate
        referrals, etc. Also: How professional staff are evaluated; review
        of documents used in evaluation

2 pm   Systems [Assoc. Director of Libraries]
        Review of systems issues, including background and future
        plans; staff introductions; hardware & software, OBIS, campus
        networking, LAN, etc.

Thursday, August 31
        Classes begin, regular reference hours & schedule begin

Sixth Week

(Monday, September 4 - Labor Day)

Tuesday, September 5

    11 am   Introduction to microform collections, locations, equipment [ref dept member]

•

Micscellaneous Stuff

Please schedule the following session with the Art Librarian (x8635), at your mutual convenience: Art Library & intro. to Library Forum. Meet at the Art Library in the Allen Art Museum annex, 2nd floor. Tour, staff introductions, overview of activities, collection strengths, major reference tools, appropriate referrals, etc. Introduction to Library Forum: what it is, what it does, who's on it.

Free time: during your first weeks here you'll have many hours that aren't otherwise scheduled, so that you'll have time to settle into your office, and generally get to know the library. Some specific suggestions: take some time to familiarize yourself with the reference collection - while many of the sources will already be familiar to you, inevitably there will be sources, and subject areas, which you'll want to spend some time getting to know. If there are sources or subject areas to which you would like a more extensive introduction, just let Jessica know and she'll arrange a meeting with the appropriate staff person (or you can arrange yourself, if you would prefer). Also, please do spend time further familiarizing yourself with any electronic resources that are new to you (Lexis/Nexis, FirstSearch, UnCover, some of our CD's, both networked & standalone, etc.), and ASK if you want some additional crash courses!

Note: the Computing Center offers "short courses" on Word, which you might want to take if you're new to Word; they will also be offering classes on Oberlin Online (the College's WWW site) and HTML - you may also want to sign up for these. [Name] in the Computing Center can let you know when the next scheduled classes are - you will need to register with her.

Wellesley College - Clapp Library

CHECKLIST FOR ORIENTING LIBRARIANS TO REFERENCE

"RefStaff" - meetings (Sept.,Jan.,May + workshops)
         - e-mail distribution list for meetings; goodies
Schedules -
    Daily = must check; initials at left - Ref Desk person
    Team+JC's calendar
    Lib research sessions list

Ref desk -
    Workstation protocols
    Phone protocols - Answer both Docs and Ref
                    - Use your name or not
                    - Transfer calls (see list on pull-out shelf)
    Multi-line phone information in file in drawer
    Info cards in center desk drawer
    College directory in drawer for security

Ref desk area -
    Reference Manual
         Esp. access policy (NB: policy posted at Circ also)
    RefStaff Notes
    Gov Docs notebook
    BLC Handbook
    etc...

    Area Libraries (and special resources) info box

    Pam files for quick info re. Wellesley et al

    Bibliographies (blue notebooks; also course-related in Info Files)

    Handouts shelves
         Esp. hours, how to dialin, campus maps....

Phone books, etc.
    CD-ROM version

BLCULS on microfiche vs. BLC InforSource on PAC

R&IS files -
    Keys board
    Letters of Intro (NB: Harvard)   --> holders for Ref Desk
    BLC card applications
         BLC special relationships:
                 On-site use for most students
                 Honors/Independent study
                 MIT reciprocity instead of BLC
                 OK for any student needing:
                     Brandeis - Jewish Studies; Middle East studies
                     BU - African Studies

Ref Info files
     Wellesley folders
     Boston maps folder

New Reference books shelf - for your current awareness (cleared wkly)

Boxes of forms -
    ILL to spike (note online version)
    Orders to Acq. box (note online version)
    Spec. Coll. procedures

Collection -
    Floor plan
    Return shelves

    Index tables (dummies)
    Atlas shelving - for folio sizes only
    Folio (dummies)

    Dictionaries on stands
    Zip Code directory on stand

    Dictionaries, Turabian, MLA on Reserve
    College cats on fiche (graduate schools, see Careers library)

    Loaning Ref items

Retrieving items from t.s. for users
    IN PROCESS
    IN REPAIR
    Incomplete serials

Directories -
    Lobby
    Near stairwells
    Beside PAC's

Emergencies -

    Language Lab:
        If no student staff there, do NOT give out emergency key at Circ.

    Copier breakdowns:
        Authorize loans of journals for copying at Schneider/Science
            User to leave ID with Circ

    "Problem patrons" - ANYONE can be asked to leave; report to campus
                            police

    EMERGENCIES notebook
    DISASTER MANUAL

    Fire alarm:
        Leave building immediately; do not wait to warn others
        Circ staff will make necessary calls, clear lobby barriers

Interlibrary Loan -
    Pick up and return routines

Participation in selecting for Reference collection --> t.s. shelf

Microforms -   [see Joan C]

    Note fiche shelved within Ref (Religion Index, Anthropological Index, etc.)
    Reading machines
    Reader-printers
        Circ/guards responsibility
    Shelving arrangements for film, fiche
    Significant sets....

U.S. Docs   [see Claire]

International Docs   "
  Shelving arrangements

REFERENCE DESK / PATRON SERVICE DOCUMENTS

Le Moyne College
Le Moyne College Library
Syracuse, New York
Memorandum

Ohio Wesleyan University
L.A. Beeghly Library
Delaware, Ohio
Reference Desk Training Checklist

Plattsburgh State College – State University of New York
Feinberg Library
Plattsburgh, New York
Guidelines for Reference Desk Service

Wellesley College
Clapp Library
Wellesley, Massachusetts
Reference Manual – Index
RefStaff Notebook – Table of Contents

William Paterson College
Askew Library
Wayne, New Jersey
Reference Department Orientation
Possible Reference Questions
Ready Reference
Some Commonly Asked (Non)-Reference Questions

MEMORANDUM

SUBJECT: Reference question negotiation

Determining whether a question is reference or directional is dependent on the interviewing process. The reference interview is often the most important function you have at the reference desk. I would like to go over this process with you in writing, and then at a later date when we have time we will go over it orally.

To begin with, please keep in mind that a person can only ask about what one knows--in other words, I will phrase my question based on what I already know. What this means is that what one asks is frequently not what one really wants to know. (I frequently give in to the temptation to ask "what do you <u>really</u> want to know?") **Never** assume that what they ask is what they need.

"Does this answer your question?" Always end the the interview with this question, and then let them know that if this information is not sufficient, they should come back to the reference desk.

Example: I know that the address and phone number of a company I need to contact would be in that city's phone book, so I ask for the phone book of that city. When you show me where the phone books are, but I do not find that city, or I find the city but not the company, I leave without the information I needed. In this case, I did not know that there are directories of companies (other ways of finding the same information), and you did not ask me what I really needed.

Example: I am writing a twenty-page paper about Torquemada, and I already know what Readers' Guide is and how to use it, so I ask you where it is. But when you show it to me, even asking if I know how to use it, I do not find anything on the man, and leave without my information.

Example: My professor told me to look up some articles on management by objectives in <u>Business Week</u>, <u>Management Focus</u>, and <u>Management Review</u>, so I ask you only where these journals are and you send me upstairs. After a frustrating three hours, I leave with only one article.

Example: I have just used MOHOC for an hour and not found anything current on my topic, and very little in this library, so I ask you how I can get books out of SU's library.

I hope the following guidelines will help you determine what the patron needs.

To begin, always answer the question first. If they ask where something is, tell them. Do not answer a question with a question. If it is an obvious directional question (facilities, person, etc.), wait to make sure they understand, and that they have no more questions.

If the question is a reference question, first answer the question as they asked it, then begin the interviewing process. What you need is enough information to get them the information they need. There are no rules or formulas for this, much of it is based on instinct and experience. It may be a simple matter of not understanding the phrasing of the question or of a language problem. Listen carefully and rephrase if necessary to make sure that you understand. Watch for body language. (I know, I know, you're not psychology majors!)

If it becomes apparent that what they ask for is not going to satisfy their needs, then you must question them in order to gather enough information to get them to the most efficient source.

EXAMPLES

Question: Where are the education journals?
Answer: The journals are located in three areas: current periodicals, Media Services, and bound periodicals. Are you looking for a specific title? Do you have a citation?
> The response to your answer may be yes, no, or maybe. The patron may say "I just need to look at some education journals, not any one in particular." In this case, you would respond that our journals are in alphabetical order, not in order by subject, so it would help to provide the patron with titles (some subject area lists are available in the Reference filing cabinet under the subject area). If the patron responds with "Yes, I have some titles" then you can direct him/her to the Serials Holdings List to find exact locations. BUT if the patron responds with "No, I don't have any titles or citations, but I need some articles on teaching reading." this is your cue to direct the patron to the proper index.

Question: Do you have any books on Shakespeare?
Answer: Yes, we do. Are you looking for books about him, such as biographies, or are you looking for information about a specific work?

Question: We don't have any books on North American Indian religions, so I have to go to SU to get them. Can you give me a pass?

Answer: Only a librarian can issue a borrower's pass to SU, so you would need to come back when one is on the desk. However, you can use the materials in Bird Library without a pass. In fact you need to talk to (give the name of the appropriate librarian by consulting the list of subject areas). But maybe we can get started here, what did you look under in the card catalog? (check the LC Subject Headings Lists, the appropriate indices, and MOHOC)

Warning: many patrons who want to go to SU will resist this process.

Question: Where is the New York Times?

Answer: Most of the issues are at Media Services, current issues still in paper, and back issues on microfilm. Are you looking for a specific day?

If the patron responds that he/she needs the issues that covered the Los Angeles riots last year, then an index is needed to make the search short: the Newspaper Abstracts on the green terminal indexes the NYT. If the patron needs articles on the inauguration last week, then an index is not going to help, but the dates are easily verified and then the patron can go directly to those days' papers.

Question: Which computer do I use to find information on Khruschev and the Berlin Wall?

Answer: The indices on the computers may not help you for an historical topic, let me show you where the best sources will be. Keep in mind that our patrons like to use the CD indices, and think they are the answer to all their questions and needs. It may be that they will in fact find a few articles on almost any topic, but going back to the guidelines for questioning, if they need more than one article, there are often better sources for several disciplines (history, literature, religious studies). You need to work with them showing them how to use the sources and showing them that there are many more sources in the print sources than on CD, and you need to make this as painless as possible (i.e. you are going to sound like your mother coaxing you to do something you didn't want to do).

REFERENCE QUESTIONS

1. Who said "The way to a man's heart is through his stomach."?

2. Do we own a French Bible?

   A new revised version of the Oxford English Bible?

3. I need some help with Shakespeare's <u>Henry IV Part I</u>.

4. I got this book out of Simon--how do I get it?

5. You don't own this journal--where can I go to get it?

6. When was the Ted Kennedy accident at Chappaquiddick? and where can I find some articles about it?

7. Where can I find current issues of <u>US News and World Report</u>?

   Last month's <u>New York Times</u>?

8. Where can I find this case:
        61 TCM 2187

9. Where can I find general information on the Brown vs Board of Education of Topeka, KS Supreme Court case?

10. Do you have a thesaurus I can use?

11. I need some general statistics on India: population, GNP, etc.

12. Where are your education journals?

13. I need to go to SU to get some books on Buddhism and they said I need a pass. Can you give me one?

14. I need some information about Alice Walker.

15. I want to write a paper about the Los Angeles riots this summer. Where can I find information?

16. Which computer can I use to find information on sensory deprivation?

17. I need some information about Rousseau.

18. Do you have an encyclopedia or something that will give me some general information about lasers?

Reference Desk Training Checklist

1. Read and discuss with Paul Burnam the Reference Philosophy and Procedures as well as the Opening/Closing Checklists. Review assertive reference style and teamwork.

2. Begin observing Reference Desk activity. Session with Paul Burnam on routine opening and closing, statistics, phones, referrals, O.S.U. courtesy borrowing, periodical lists of other libraries, common referrals.

3. Tour the general Physical Plant of Beeghly, the branches, and the campus as a whole. Begin to know the student body and faculty of Ohio Wesleyan, especially frequent library users like ENG105 students, research methods classes, etc. Paul

4. Learn the common directional queries including:
   *the general location of collections in Beeghly and branches; how to use LCSH and LC call numbers.
   *operation of photocopiers, microform reader/printers, telephones, computer printers, Microlab questions, and other routine equipment in Beeghly. Paul, Bernard, and/or Sarah.

5. Introduction to III and typical online catalog reference questions. Review basic OPAC searches. Paul

6. Typical periodicals related questions. Paul

7. Classmate one-on-one training with Julie McDaniel. Attend CLASSMATE workshop.

8. Government Documents:
   a) Marcive introduction with Paul
   b) Government Documents review with Paul. Commonly used sources, quirks of SuDocs numbers, etc.

9. PsycLIT introduction with Tom Green.

10. OCLC/FirstSearch training. Julie

11. Internet resources introduction. Paul or Julie

12. Reference Collection: Quirks of arrangement, frequently used sources. All librarians contribute.

13. ILL introduction with Sarah Bergman.

14. Unusual features of telephone calls at the Reference Desk. How to access phonemail at the

Reference Desk. Paul

15. Activity during slow periods (e.g., professional reading, exploring Internet, *Choice* cards, examining new Reference books, etc.)

This checklist assumes Janis is already familiar with:
        *basic reference interviewing techniques
        *common reference books and periodical indexes
        *different approaches to typical term paper research
        *fundamentals of online searching

GUIDELINES FOR REFERENCE DESK SERVICES

The purpose of these guidelines is to communicate Feinberg Library expectations for librarians staffing the Reference Desk. The guidelines are meant to convey the sense of what we hope to accomplish and, in a few general examples, suggestions how to do it. The guidelines are not intended as a procedures manual for all occasions but as an aid to the professional judgments librarianship frequently requires. Specific and more detailed reference policies and procedures are included in the appendix to these guidelines.

1. Service Objectives

The primary objective and highest priority of the Reference Desk is to determine the information needs of individual Plattsburgh State student, faculty, and staff users who come to Feinberg Library and to assist them in using library resources to meet those needs, or to refer them to other sources or locations as appropriate. The needs of these users take precedence over all other activities that may take place at the Desk or other forms of user communication (telephone, email, etc.).

Meeting high standards of Reference Desk Service includes:

Exercising initiative, judgment, courtesy and flexibility in meeting the needs of library users

Offering active, not passive, assistance to users

Not leaving the Reference Desk area unattended or out of sight for more than a few (3-4) minutes

Making special efforts when dealing with foreign or disabled users

Following up on questions when possible ("Did you find the answer?")

Not using Reference Desk hours for student appointments, brief (or lengthy) meetings with other staff members, conversations, etc.

2. Desk Ambience

Often the first impression of the library is influenced by what the user sees and hears at a service point, such as the Reference Desk. Preserving a good public image and establishing a good rapport with library users is thus a responsibility of everyone at the Desk. The image we portray affects the public's perception of the Library and its services as a whole.

A good public image and good rapport include:

Having an approachable demeanor and a personal appearance that is in good taste

Acknowledging newcomers in a friendly and receptive way

Avoiding an appearance of being buried in paperwork, engaged in telephone conversation, or distracted by personal contacts

Keeping the desk area between you and patrons as clear and neat as possible to avoid the physical barriers that make one less approachable to the public; work brought to the desk should be minimal and not require significant concentration

Presenting a positive, enthusiastic public service attitude that responds to requests with courtesy and promptness

3. Room Ambience

Reference Room ambience should be conducive to asking and answering questions and comfortable for doing research. Use of the Reference Room by librarians for negotiating queries and by large numbers of students for research purposes often requires tolerance as well as control of varying degrees of sound levels. Common sense and respect for everyone's need to concentrate should be the guiding principle in estimating the suitable voice level necessary for negotiating queries and conducting research.

Creating an ambience conducive to effective use of Reference Room services and resources includes:

Keeping everyone's voice level subdued, a notch or two below the normal, so that both communication and concentration can take place

Advising visiting groups and orientation tours to respect the needs of Reference Room users for concentration and minimal disruption of activities

Discouraging college instructors from holding classes and lecturing in the Reference Room; providing alternative rooms for such purposes and releasing the needed sources to them for an hour or so

Enforcing the Library's food and drink policy evenly by all staff to minimize abuse; strict enforcement of no food or drink policy, regardless of containers, in areas with computer equipment, such as the ESC

Observing the Library's policy of not bringing food or any liquid containers to service desks, such as the Reference Desk or student ESC Desk.

Polite, firm, and swift intervention by the librarian at the Reference Desk to maintain a pleasant working atmosphere and the balance between the need to communicate and concentrate

4. Telephone Issues

The Reference Desk will provide telephone patrons with the normal range of information services characterized as *Directional* or *Brief Reference* questions. However, in accord with the objectives stated in (1), users waiting at the desk have priority over callers (or email queries). In addition, patrons with questions requiring *In-depth* research or lengthy telephone answers should either be advised to come to the library or the librarian should handle the question as a follow-up procedure after leaving the Reference Desk.

Proper Reference Desk telephone use includes:

Prompt and courteous service; when answering the telephone, identify the unit: "Feinberg Library Reference Desk. This is (name). May I help you?"

Keeping the line as open as possible and reserved for information questions only; not tying up the line with lengthy answers, long conversations--personal or professional, or having your personal office phone calls transferred to the desk while on duty

Discouraging patrons from using the Reference Desk phone, except in an emergency

Not keeping a patron waiting at the Reference Desk due to a telephone query; the query needs to be completed immediately or a follow-up arranged as soon as you are free again

Not interrupting work with a patron to answer the phone; phone transfer (after five rings) should be to the Reference Department line (5191) or to an answering machine when the Reference secretary is unavailable.

5. Statistics

Library data gathering for Information and Instructional Services serves both in-house and SUNY Central purposes. Each year SUNY Central collects specific library data which is gathered and published in a *Statistical Release*. Except for the bibliographic instruction category, the categories on our statistics gathering sheet correspond exactly to State requirements. State definitions are provided for some of the categories, but not for all of them. The definitions suggested below take the State guidelines into consideration.

Directional Questions: *responses involving the location of places in the Library or on campus; these questions do not involve reference sources*

Brief (Quick) Reference Questions: *any search of either a bibliographic or abstracting and indexing source (print or CD-ROM)* which takes _less than 5 minutes_ to accomplish; quick, casual, on-demand retrieval of information

In-depth Questions: any search of a bibliographic or abstracting and indexing source (print or CD-ROM) which _exceeds 5 minutes_ in length; questions that requires a sustained search effort

Bibliographic Instruction Questions: responses to substantive questions involving the Introduction to Library Research course should not include directional queries related to the course (record those in the Directional Questions category). Please note: while librarians should not be expected to answer LIB101 questions for students, they should provide friendly help deciphering assignments whenever possible (to the same extent this is done for students in other courses). When the assignment is not clear to the librarian or if the student appears to need special assistance, he/she should be referred to the course (section) instructor.

6. Staffing and Scheduling

Librarians from all units of the Library serve at the Reference Desk. The desk schedule is established before the semester break and begins and ends on the first and last days of the semester. Staff members are queried for preferences and the times they are unavailable as a result of professional commitments. Efforts are made to assign hours (and evenings) fairly and on rotation. A draft schedule is drawn up and adjusted as necessary. The Head of Information and Instructional Services serves as _Desk Coordinator_ and prepares the schedule, assigning changes or adjustments as necessary. Each semester and summer a reference librarian will be appointed as a backup in this role.

To Make Scheduling Work Smoothly Each Staff Member Is Responsible For:

Arranging changes in the schedule that involve trading time to accommodate for planned absences (days off, vacations, conferences, etc.)

Recording all schedule changes arranged independently on the calendar at the Reference Desk

Contacting the Desk Coordinator (or backup) in cases of illness or unexpected, important meetings or other unplanned professional commitments requiring a brief change of schedule; the Desk Coordinator would find a substitute in a fair and equitable manner from librarians available; the expectation is that a one or two day absence would involve a "payback" of time but that a longer absence would not; the Desk Coordinator would ensure the fair distribution of desk coverage in these cases by spreading workload throughout the librarian ranks.

(Approved by the Library Faculty, March 1993)

WELLESLEY COLLEGE LIBRARY

REFERENCE MANUAL

Index

refman:index.txt

```
             Wellesley College - Clapp Library

                    RefStaff Notebook
                    -----------------


                    TABLE OF CONTENTS



     -  Current Assignments distributed by Faculty
             Annotated for best sources of answers

     -  Service Policies
             New or Highlights

     -  CD-ROM notes

     -  Library Strategy Research Sessions (request forms)

     -  Reference resources
             New or Highlights

     -  Lists of faculty, new faculty, faculty on leave, etc.

     -  E-Mail distributed to RefStaff in past year

     -  New subject headings added to catalog

     - Campus Wide Information System (CWIS) Web server
             What's new

     -  Lexis/Nexis notes

     - Clapp Library floor plans




refs:refstaff-notebook.lst
```

It's always a good idea to start the reference interview with open questions to allow the patron an opportunity to express his/her question more fully without having the librarian put words in the patron's mouth. Attached are some suggested questions for both exploring the information need and for guiding the patron/student to closure.

Reference Department
Orientation
1994

REFERENCE DEPARTMENT
ORIENTATION

CHECKLIST FOR SELF-GUIDED TOUR

Library

First Floor

<u>General</u>

    Copiers - 3 locations
        Enlarging/reducing copier
        Staff copier
    Change Machines
    Copy Card Vending Machines
    Elevators
    Emergency exits
    Fire Alarms
    Keys
    Microfiche Reader/Printer
    Pencil Sharpener
    Periodicals Printouts
    Public Access Catalog (ASK_Q)
        Locations - Reference area, AV area, Curriculum Materials
    Restrooms
    Sorting shelves (preshelving)
    Staff Room
        Refrigerator, microwave
        Transparency maker
    Stairs
    Water fountain

<u>Lobby</u>

    Restrooms
    Telephones
    No campus phone yet (ask at reference desk)
    Auditorium

<u>Service Desks</u>

    Circulation
        Interlibrary loan pickups/returns
    Reserves/reserve binders
    AV service desk
    Reference desk
        Interlibrary Loan requests
        Electronic Access: OCLC, Other Library Catalogs, WPC Periodicals Directory
            FirstSearch password, New Jersey Union List of Serials
    Curriculum Materials Offices
    Electronic Reference Center

Collections
      Circulating books
            A-L
            M
      Computer Software
      New Jersey Collection
      Curriculum Materials
            juvenile fiction/non-fiction, textbooks, teaching aids, reference, MAC software,
            picture books, award books, curriculum guides

      AV Collection
            films, videos, CDs, cassettes, laser disks, AV hardware, etc.

      Reference Collection
            Reference stacks, index stacks, index tables, New Jersey documents,
            encyclopedias, special tables (business, health, media,census, grants)
            ready reference, atlases, dictionary stands, reference microforms

Offices

      Lending Services
      Reference/Automation
            Temporary scanner and laser printer location
            Machine room
            CRS
      AV
      Curriculum Materials
            MAC
            Apple

Classrooms, Group studies

      Curriculum Materials Classroom
      Auditorium
      Preview rooms (AV)
      Group studies
            Curriculum Materials
            Reference "Hall" area

Second Floor
      Circulating books
            N-Z
            Oversize

Basement (Not open)
      Instruction room (Still in wing 233)
            Publications Storage
            Transparency files
      Special Collections (still in Storage)
      Restrooms

Wayne Hall

Second Floor
Periodicals Collection

Magazines, journals, newspapers, ERIC microfiche
Periodicals Service Desk
WPC Periodicals Directory - Online
Microform Reader/Printers
Copiers
Change Machines
Copy Card Vending Machine
Reading Room
Interlibrary Loan Office

First Floor
Director's Office
Director's Secretary
Mailboxes
Fax

Hunziker Wing

Collection development
Ordering and receiving
Cataloging
Instruction Room (BI classroom, publications storage, transparencies)

Matelson Basement

Old Indexes
Oversize Reference
Old periodicals
Chinese language materials
Special collections (first editions)
Mansells
Old reference microforms

January 1995

POSSIBLE REFERENCE QUESTIONS

Open Questions

1. Can you tell me more?
2. Would you elaborate?
3. Can you give me an example?
4. Can you be more specific?
5. Can you give me some background information or context?
6. Can you define what you mean by _____ for me?
7. Can you give me some sense of how much information you need?
8. Where have you looked already?
9. Do you have a thesis statement? Can you state it for me?
10. I'm not sure what is meant by _____, can you give me a definition or a description?
11. Can you explain what you mean by _____?
12. That sounds like a big project, can you be more specific?
13. So what you're saying is .....
14. What did the professor ask you to do/what did the professor say about the assignment?
15. That's a very interesting topic, can you tell me more?

Narrowing Questions

1. Is this for a class, presentation, paper, etc...?
2. Does it matter when the material was published?
3. Do you need recent information or doesn't it matter?
4. Do you want to use periodical literature or books or both?
5. Did your professor state that you need to use certain types of sources? such as journals, professional literature, statistical ?
6. Do you need to find articles in popular magazines or do you need to use research studies?
7. This van be a very multidisciplinary topic. I can see several ways to go with this. Are you interested in finding articles from a particular perspective? medical? sociological? educational? consumer-oriented?
8. How much time do you have?
9. These are the kinds of articles you find in Infotrac or _____, is this what you want?
10. Do you have your assignment sheet?
11. Do you need brief information or something more involved?
12. Have you already looked in _____?
13. How does this look? Is this what you want?

READY REFERENCE

"Ready reference" refers to reference sources used so frequently by the reference librarian that the sources are kept at the reference desk. "Ready reference" sources do not circulate and must be used in the library. Patrons who wish to use these sources away from the reference desk, must leave an ID card at the reference desk. Ready reference sources should have "book cards" so that the ID can be attached to the card and left at the reference desk. If the book card is missing, use a scrap card or similar piece of paper instead. Although exceptions are rare, the reference librarian may occasionally allow a patron to take a reference book out of the library for a short period of time.

Following are a list of questions along with a likely source in which to locate an answer. Feel free to experiment and determine if the same question can be answered in more than one source.

What is the population of Mexico? (World Almanac)

When is Sadie Hawkins day? (Chase's)

How do I cite a magazine article? (Turabian's Manual of Style)

How do I cite using APA style? (APA Style Manual)

What is the address of Common Cause? (Washington Information Directory)

Where is Hispaniola? (Goode's World Atlas)

What was the inflation rate in 1992? (Statistical Abstract of the US)

What is the number of households in Newark, N.J? (City and County Data Book)

How can I write to MADD? (Encyclopedia of Associations)

How many square miles is the town of Ridgewood, N.J. (N.J. Municipal Data Book)

What is the phone number for the US Copyright Office? (US Government Manual)

What is the definition of habeas corpus? (Black's Law Dictionary)

Where is Dartmouth College?   (HEP Higher Education Directory)

Who is the superintendent of the Paterson school district?
 (N.J. School Directory)

What do the letters RADAR stand for?   (Abbreviations, Acronyms and Initialisms)

What is the drug Trimox used for?   (PDR)

Find the address of Simon & Shuster.   (Literary Market Place)

How can I subscribe to the publication Wired? (Ulrichs)

Where is there a description of courses in the Biology Department?
   (WPC College Catalogs)

Is the book "Generation X" still in print? (Books in Print)

Are there any daily newspapers in St. Petersburg, Florida? (Gale Directory
   of Publications)

What is the zip code for Fairbanks, Alaska?   (US ZipCode Directory)

Who is the author of the "Closing of the American Mind"? (Author
   guide to Books in Print)

Askew Library
Reference Department
Jan-95

SOME COMMONLY ASKED (NON)-REFERENCE QUESTIONS

IT SHOULD BE CLEAR FROM THE ANSWERS TO THESE QUESTIONS THAT WE
ERR ON THE SIDE OF GENEROSITY IF POSSIBLE.

1. Where's the pencil sharpener?
    Electric sharpener is at the ref desk. Sharpeners will be
    placed in the copier room and in other locations not yet
    determined.

2. Can I have a paper clip/white out/scissors? A stapler?
    Ruler? These items should be in the reference desk drawer
    and students may borrow. Notify Kim if supplies are low
    or items are missing.

3. Can I borrow a pen/pencil?
    There are always golf pencils around. You can lend a pen.
    Lend your own pen at your own risk.

4. Do you have any paper I can use?
    Use scrap paper from Cds. There's also scrap paper at the
    PAC terminals.

5. Do you have envelopes?
    We only have campus envelopes and letterhead.

6. Calculators?
    No. Lend your own at your own risk. Don't leave your
    calculator in the reference desk.

7. Where are the copy machines?
    In the copy room? Behind the M's.

8. Where is the copier/enlarger?
    This is being relocated from the second floor to ?

9. Do you have any change?
    There are $1 change machines in the copy room. There are no
    change machines for larger denominations on campus. There
    are vendacard machines - you can buy $1, $5, $10 and $20
    cards. First time use of the card costs 30 cents. 10
    cents per page. Give out your own change if you want.
    There are no places to get change for large denominations
    unless you buy something at the student center or
    on weekends at one of the nearby stores.

10. Can I use your telephone?
    Once on campus phones are installed - no. There are public
    pay phones in the lobby area and on-campus phones will be
    installed.

11. Where are the restrooms? Drinking fountains?
    Restrooms are in the outer lobby area and near the index

tables.　There will be rest rooms on the second floor when the building is finished.　Water fountain is near entrance to AV.

12. Are there typewriters?
There are no typewriters for students.　Students can type papers at any of the multipurpose computer labs on campus -usually the Coach House.　The computers in the electronic lab are for library use.　There is no word processing software on them.

13. Can I bring my own computer in the library?　Yes, however until the library is finished, there are few outlets available.　There is one in the room where the encyclopedias are.

14. Do I need a WPC ID card to use the library? (to get a periodical? for a reserve book?)

Anyone can use the library.　An ID card is necessary to check out a book. In order to obtain a periodical any form of ID is accepted.　Similarly, to use a ready reference book, any form of ID is accepted.　A book on reserve for a class will probably have to be used in sight of the Lending Services Desk.

15. My class isn't where it's supposed to be -what do I do?

Is this a BI class?　If so, check reference schedule. Most BI classes are in Wing 233,　Curriculum Materials BI classes are in the Library.

If not BI, check schedule, call department, give patron department phone number.　Sometimes there's nothing we can do.

16. Do you have this textbook?　Check PAC.　Usually no, the library does not purchase textbooks routinely.

17. Where can I get a cup of coffee, food, etc.?　There are vending machines in the student center, snack bar in the student center but not weekends.　7-eleven?

18. Can you find my son?　It's an emergency.

There is no paging system.　In most cases no, but use your discretion if you think it's a real emergency.

19. Do you have a hole punch?

There's one at Lending Services and in Curriculum Materials.

20. The copier isn't working, took my dime, is making poor copies....
    Refer the patron to lending services.

21. There's something wrong with the PAC,

    Try to help. Put an out of order sign on the station.
    Inform Automation Dept.

22. The printer in the lab isn't working.

    If there's no lab assistant, it is the reference librarian's
    responsibility to check out problems in the lab. In most
    cases, you should be able to fix it.

                              To be continued!

                              Fall 1994

LIBRARY INSTRUCTION DOCUMENTS

Harding University
Brackett Library
Searcy, Arizona
The Teaching Model

Plattsburgh State College – State University of New York
Feinberg Library
Plattsburgh, New York
*Appendix A – Objectives for Introduction to Library
Research (LIB 101)*

Since bibliographic instruction is part of reference service, librarians are also expected to be competent teachers.

THE TEACHING MODEL

teachers are expected to demonstrate the following characteristics:

1. Instructional Content
   a. Current knowledge of discipline
   b. Knowledge of specific course content
   c. Integration of current knowledge into the classroom
2. Instructional Design
   a. Selecting the appropriate objectives that reflect:
      (1) Expected content of course
      (2) Appropriate level of learner
      (3) Appropriate level of difficulty of course
      (4) A variety of thinking skills, i.e.:
         (a) Knowledge
         (b) Comprehension
         (c) Application
         (d) Analysis
         (e) Synthesis
         (f) Evaluation
   b. Planning - Teacher demonstrates preparation through:
      (1) Up-to-date bibliographies
      (2) Visuals
      (3) Demonstrations
   c. Integrating faith and learning
   d. Instructional Delivery
      (1) Christian role model
      (2) Caring, respectful, concerned attitude
      (3) Enthusiastic about subjects
      (4) Effective delivery
         (a) Maintaining focus of learner
         (b) Rapport
         (c) Interaction with students through encouraging student's questions and comments
         (d) Speaks in expressive manner with clarity and proper volume and pace
   e. Instructional management
      (1) Scheduling
      (2) Planning lecture content with instructor
      (3) Evaluate and revise lecture

Librarians also are responsible for maintaining up-to-date, detailed procedure and/or policy manuals for their areas of responsibility. Taken as a group, these manuals constitute a major portion of the Library Manual which documents library operational procedures hand policies.

APPENDIX A

OBJECTIVES FOR INTRODUCTION TO LIBRARY RESEARCH (LIB101)

DEFINITIONS AND ORGANIZATION OF INFORMATION

"The user understands how information is defined by experts, and recognizes how that knowledge can help determine the direction of his/her search for specific information."

> The student will be introduced to information types and will understand that there are different formats (books/periodicals/electronic/other, including friends, etc.); different sources (primary/ secondary); and different qualities (subjective/objective or analytical/factual).

> The student will recognize that information is organized using different systems for different types (see types above). Some systems of organization are derived from the subject/discipline relationship.

TOPIC ANALYSIS

"Once a topic of interest is selected, the user understands how it can be refined and can formulate a question."

> The student will understand that it may be necessary to rework her/his topic to fit organization schemes: subject/ discipline, etc. Reworking the topic may include developing terminology appropriate to the topic and to the search to be carried out.

> The student will recognize that the subject/discipline relationship will affect his/her topic: the same topic may be handled differently in different disciplines, and some topics are always interdisciplinary.

ACCESS: PRESENTATION OF INFORMATION

"The user understands that there are [sic] a variety of information sources called access tools whose primary purpose is to identify other information sources through the use of access points."

> The student will understand that information needed to identify information sources is arranged into citations and will recognize

the elements in these citations and where citations typically occur.

The student will recognize that access points are needed to search for information and that the citation elements of author and title are access points that can also be used for evaluating information.

The student will recognize that access sources vary by subject area and by type of information that the sources include.

The student may be introduced to the value of unrecorded sources, that in some disciplines there may exist an "invisible college" of information communicated among experts through informal channels.

ACCESS: CONTROLLED VOCABULARIES

"The user understands that some sources use controlled vocabulary assigned by an indexer, cataloger, or computer programmer as access points. ... The rules governing indexing practices may influence the process of retrieval."

The student will understand what a controlled vocabulary is, how the subject/discipline relationship will affect the terms in the vocabulary, that the formats of controlled vocabularies may differ, and how the use of a controlled vocabulary affects information research.

The student will recognize how using a controlled vocabulary in a search differs from free-text searching.

ACCESS: THE SEARCH PROCESS

The user understands how to construct an approach or strategy appropriate to the anticipated result of the research process."

The student will recognize that the criteria of the end product, i.e., intended audience, type of project, purpose of assignment, determine the information need and therefore the information search.

The student will understand that there may be a lack of recorded information and that this can be either an indication to stop research on the initial topic and refocus or change the topic, or it can indicate a need to do original research, depending on the nature of the project.

The student will understand that the relevance of information retrieved to the project's particular needs should be evaluated throughout the research process and may shape the process itself.

EVALUATION OF INFORMATION

"The user can evaluate the citation retrieved or the accessed information and determine whether or not it is ... appropriate."

The student will understand how to evaluate materials based on the analysis of her/his information need.

The student will understand the purpose for references in his/her own work as well as in that of published authors (plagiarism). The student understands how the inclusion of references in information can be used to help evaluate the information.

The student will recognize the need for style manuals to assure consistency in citation formats.

GLOSSARY

citation: a bibliographic record that includes the information necessary to retrieve an information source; see also "Reference" below.

discipline: a branch of knowledge, esp. one of several broad areas of knowledge that include numerous more specific subject fields (see "Subject" below). Usually there are three disciplines discussed in information research: the Natural Sciences, the Social Sciences and the Humanities.

reference: a bibliographic record that includes the information necessary to retrieve an information source, often used synonymously with "citation" (see above).

source: a physical entity in any medium upon which is recorded information. There are sources that are used during information research and sources that are the end result of information research, the former often called "research sources" or "access sources" or "access tools."

subject: a field of knowledge as a course of study, e.g., education, criminology, physics, etc. See also "Topic" below.

subject/discipline relationship: the hierarchical arrangement of knowledge whereby subject fields are included in broad discipline groupings

topic: the subject or theme information research, to be distinguished from "subject" (as defined above) by virtue of the fact that in information research a topic falls within a subject field, e.g., environmental science may be the subject of the topic, "acid rain."

LIAISON / OUTREACH SERVICES DOCUMENTS

Willamette University
Mark O. Hatfield Library
Salem, Oregon
Librarian – Faculty Liaison Notes
Faculty – Librarian Liaison Program

Librarian-Faculty Liaison Notes

Several librarians have asked for some guidance as to what to discuss with their departments. Here's what I have come up with so far:

Call department chair and arrange to attend a department meeting.

Agenda

explanation: 1) faciliate communication and cooperation.
2) work together to improve the library's collections & services.

logistics: 1) who will be the faculty liaison (department chair).
2) when to meet (beginning of each year; after that, as needed).

responsibilites of the liaisons: see below

librarian liaison:

*send all Choice cards to department chair to distribute
*inform faculty of new resources acquired that may interest the dep't
*consult faculty about weeding, evaluation of journal collection, other collection
  development questions
*encourage those departments (or faculty) not using library instruction to consider
  doing so
*inform faculty of problems their students may be having in finding materials or in
  understanding an assignment
*find out what faculty expect/want from the library and how we can better assist them
  and their students
*inform faculty of new library developments
*meet with candidates for faculty positions, show them the library, etc.
*meet with new faculty if desired to discuss library instruction, collection development,
  library procedures, etc.
*develop our own interests/depth in a given academic discipline
*establish connection with department members and find out what's happening in the
  department

Faculty:

*return Choice cards and all other book orders to library liaison
*inform library liaison of your individual research interests
*discuss new course ideas with library liaison
*explore questions or concerns about the collection/collection development
*inform library liaison of class assignments and projects that will require heavy use of
  the library
*make suggestions, offer ideas, keep librarian informed of departmental developments
*find out what's happening at the library and what the library can do for you

Remind/reassure faculty that all librarians will continue to do reference and library
instruction across disciplines??

FACULTY-LIBRARIAN LIAISON PROGRAM

Who should the liaison librarian meet with?
>   *invite ourselves to a department meeting at the start of each year, explain program, faculty liaison will be department chair unless they wish to appoint someone else as faculty liaison, anyone else from the dept. is encouraged to chat with the library liaison at anytime

How often should the liaison meet?
>   *meet with whole department at least once a year and then as needed and/or desired

What do we want to accomplish?
>   *establish cooperation and communication
>   *can meet with new faculty individually if desired to explain library procedures or privileges and discuss research interests
>   *discuss library instruction, why it's valuable, how to schedule, etc.
>   *encourage suggestions and new ideas for the library
>   *discuss class assignments and projects and new course ideas
>   *explore collection development questions and problems (establish new patterns so that if a faculty person is ordering odd stuff, the liaison librarian could meet with that individual to discuss the situation)
>   *discover areas of research for each faculty member in a department
>   *find out what faculty expect/want from the library and how we can better assist them and their students
>   *inform faculty of new library developments
>   *inform faculty of problems their students may be having in finding materials (i.e. botanist info. last semester) or in understanding an assignment
>   *liaison librarian could meet with professors interviewing for a job and meet one-on-one with new faculty to introduce them to the library
>   *develop our own interests/depth in a given academic discipline

EVALUATION OF TRAINEE DOCUMENTS

Harding University
Brackett Library
Searcy, Arizona
Reference Service Evaluation

Tarleton State University
Dick Smith Library
Stephenville, Texas
Performance Appraisal Form

REFERENCE SERVICE EVALUATION

(To be completed by Student Reference Assistants)

Librarian being evaluated: _____

All _____ librarians share in providing reference service. All have varying expertise and experience. In an effort to improve our service to students, we would appreciate your completing this form based on your observations while working with us or being assisted by us. Any additional comments you can share would also be very helpful. Librarians will see only the compiled results.

Answers: A = Agree
          N = Neither agree nor disagree
          D = Disagree
          U = Unknown (No chance to observe)

_____ 1. This librarian is friendly and approachable to students seeking information.

_____ 2. This librarian acts interested in the questions students ask and in helping them find answers.

_____ 3. This librarian interviews the seeker to attempt to fully understand the questions being asked.

_____ 4. This librarian goes with the patron to the recommended source.

_____ 5. This librarian encourages the patron to return if he or she needs further help.

_____ 6. This librarian seems to be familiar with a wide variety of reference sources.

_____ 7. I feel this librarian likes for me to ask questions.

_____ 8. I am confident this librarian understands how to use the online catalog and the CD-ROM indexes.

_____ 9. If I, personally, needed help with a reference question and all the librarians were available, I would prefer to consult them in the order below. (1=1st, 2=2nd, etc. U=Unknown)

        _____   _____
        _____   _____
        _____   _____
        _____

Please use the back to make any other valuative comments or suggestions aimed at helping us upgrade our reference service.

LIBRARY FACULTY EVALUATION
CONTINUING SCHOLARSHIP/UNIVERSITY SERVICE
REPORT FORM FOR FACULTY PORTFOLIO

INSTRUCTIONS: A report form will be completed for each activity listed on the Faculty Member/Supervisor Annual Plan for Continuing Scholarship <u>and</u> University Service. Documentation can include such items as research summary reports, reprints of articles written, description of professional meetings attended, copies of materials developed for presentations, details of service activities, etc.

FACULTY MEMBER_____

ACTIVITY _____

DATES _____

TIME REQUIRED_____

OBJECTIVES OF ACTIVITY:_____

_____

_____

_____

_____

_____

APPLICATION/IMPLEMENTATION: _____

_____

_____

_____

_____

_____

_____

PERFORMANCE APPRAISAL FORM

EMPLOYEE'S NAME: _____ DATE: _____

DEPARTMENT:_____ TITLE: _____

PLEASE SELECT THE LETTER THAT MOST ACCURATELY APPLIES:

A Meets Position Requirements

B Some Weaknesses - Progress Adequate

C Some Weaknesses - Progress Slow

D Very Weak - Progress Inadequate

RATING FACTORS	PRIOR TO END OF 4TH MONTH	PRIOR TO END OF 6TH MONTH	OTHER MONTH:__
ATTITUDE	A _____ B _____ C _____ D _____	A _____ B _____ C _____ D _____	A _____ B _____ C _____ D _____
ATTENDANCE	A _____ B _____ C _____ D _____	A _____ B _____ C _____ D _____	A _____ B _____ C _____ D _____
QUALITY OF WORK	A _____ B _____ C _____ D _____	A _____ B _____ C _____ D _____	A _____ B _____ C _____ D _____
QUANTITY OF WORK	A _____ B _____ C _____ D _____	A _____ B _____ C _____ D _____	A _____ B _____ C _____ D _____
KNOWLEDGE OF JOB	A _____ B _____ C _____ D _____	A _____ B _____ C _____ D _____	A _____ B _____ C _____ D _____

THIS EMPLOYEE: ____ SHOULD BE RETAINED   ____ SHOULD BE DISMISSED

COMMENTS:_____

_____

_____

(ADDITIONAL COMMENTS BY SUPERVISOR OR EMPLOYEE MAY BE ATTACHED)

_____   _____

EMPLOYEE SIGNATURE   DATE   SUPERVISOR SIGNATURE   DATE

_____

DEPARTMENT HEAD SIGNATURE   DATE

(IF DISMISSAL IS RECOMMENDED, ATTACH A COPY OF THIS FORM TO THE LETTER MAKING SUCH RECOMMENDATION)

COMPREHENSIVE TRAINING DOCUMENTS

Hope College
Van Wylen Library
Holland, Michigan
Employee Handbook

Marymount University
Reinsch Library
Arlington, Virginia
Reference Department Orientation
Appendix C

University of Richmond
Boatwright Library
Richmond, Virginia
General Reference Service Guidelines and Polices
General Reference Department Service

William Paterson College
Askew Library
Wayne, New Jersey
Orientation Manual for the new Reference Librarian

Hope College

VAN WYLEN LIBRARY

* * * * * * * *

Employee Handbook

Hope College

VAN WYLEN LIBRARY

New Employee Orientation Checklist

NAME_____DEPARTMENT_____

POSITION_____STARTING DATE_____

WELCOME! We are pleased that you have joined the Hope College Van Wylen Library staff. You are an important member of our team.

During your first two months, you will be receiving information about Hope College and about your job and its importance to the Library and College community. This checklist will chart your progress in this process. It is detailed so that you may continue to refer to it whenever the need arises.

Your supervisor, _____, is responsible for scheduling these activities and seeing that they are all accomplished. Please be sure to have each person who orients you initial and date each activity. The last page must be completely signed by all necessary personnel and be maintained in your Library personnel file.

LIBRARY INFORMATION

NAME TAGS - will be ordered by the secretaries.

REQUESTED FORMS - Below are forms contained in the folder marked "Request Forms" in the secretaries' office file cabinet:

-Motor Vehicle Registration for obtaining a campus parking sticker.
-Cash Payment requests for requesting a check from the Business Office.
    Note: Must be approved and signed by David.
-Inter-departmental charge form is used when charging or crediting another department on campus. Note: Must be signed by David.
-Request for Travel Reimbursement when incurring expenses on a trip. (Green color) Note: Must be signed by David.
-Request for Authorization of Payment to a Staff or Faculty Member

The forms shown below are filed under their title in the secretaries' office file cabinet:

-Absence forms to be filled out before a planned absence. Note: Must be approved and signed by David. He then sends to the Provost for his signature.
-Work request forms to be filled out when turning work in to the secretaries.

RESEARCH GUIDES - are usually ordered in a large quantity, so when the desk area supplies becomes low, please check for an additional supply. To re-order please notify the secretaries by giving them a sample copy along with the number of copies needed. (Research guides are duplicated in the same color stock.) They will order from the campus Word Processing Center. It takes two day minimum depending on department work load.

STAFF CALENDAR - Please record your planned absences, vacations, etc., as much in advance as possible on the library system.

SUPPLIES - A cabinet of various supplies such as tape, glue sticks, staples, pens, etc. is kept in the secretaries' office. You may help yourself to any of these items but please notify the secretary if the you are taking the last one. Purchasing library and office supplies should be done through the secretaries. Please determine as exactly as possible what is needed using the Geneva Bookstore catalog and give the information to the secretary. Our student couriers will be able to pick up certain supplies on their scheduled runs.

TELEPHONE - When you will be away from your desk for awhile, your phone can be forwarded to another desk in the library or to the staff lounge. Press *3 and then the number to which you want your phone forwarded. To cancel the forward, press #3. Please notify the secretary and your supervisor if you will not be working your usual hours for that day.

WORD PROCESSING - Any copying of documents of 25 or more is done at a cost savings by the college Word Processing Department. A pink order form is completed and clipped to the orignal. It is then placed in the "Hand Delivery" basket in the library receiving room, to be taken by the courier on her/his scheduled run. Note: Please let the secretaries know when a large request is made in order to work with the courier on pick-up of items. Also, any special rush items should be marked and brought to the courier's/secretaries' attention for special handling.

HOPE COLLEGE
INSTITUTIONAL MISSION STATEMENT

AND

EXPANDED STATEMENT OF INSTITUTIONAL PURPOSE

WITH

GOALS FOR THE ACADEMIC PROGRAM

MISSION STATEMENT:

The mission of Hope College is to offer with recognized excellence, academic programs in the liberal arts, in the setting of a residential, undergraduate, coeducational college, and in the context of the historic Christian faith.

EXPANDED STATEMENT OF INSTITUTIONAL GOALS AND OBJECTIVES FOR THE ACADEMIC PROGRAM IN TERMS OF STUDENT ACHIEVEMENT

A.   Goal 1:   Students will have an ability to understand, communicate, and critically appraise differing ways of knowing.

   1.   Objective 1:   Students will possess fundamental skills which enable them to:

      a.   Read, listen, and view with sensitivity and with critical acumen.

      b.   Express themselves clearly, correctly, and succinctly in writing and speaking.

      c.   Apply mathematical principles and procedures effectively.

      d.   Use research facilities and library resources competently.

      e.   Use a studio or performance space to create or perform a work of art satisfactorily.

   2.   Objective 2:   Students will be able to make critical judgments about a fundamental body of knowledge.

HOPE COLLEGE INSTITUTIONAL MISSION STATEMENT
AND EXPANDED STATEMENT OF INSTITUTIONAL PURPOSE
WITH GOALS FOR THE ACADEMIC PROGRAM
Page Three

2. Objective 2:   All graduates will display an openness
    to the totality of human experience, always seeking an
    integration of learning, experience and faith that
    leads to a responsible, purposeful and fulfilling life.

3. Objective 3:   All graduates will have developed the
    intellectual and methodological foundations for
    lifelong learning.

4. Objective 4:   All graduates will have developed the
    intellectual and ethical foundations for a life of
    service to others.

E. Goal 5:   Each academic department and program will be
    continually improving so that all departments and
    programs will be either strong or exemplary in
    reference to criteria that Hope College will
    develop.

1. Objective 1:   The faculty and academic administration
    will regularly review current programs to determine how
    such programs could be strengthened as well as the
    academic and economic feasibility of their
    continuation.

2. Objective 2:   The College will strengthen its library
    holdings and services, while concurrently integrating
    the library more fully into the academic program.

3. Objective 3:   The excellence of our academic programs
    and facilities will be recognized by ourselves, our
    graduates, and by academicians and others outside the
    College.

JEN:ACADGOAL.NCA
Revised 11/26/91 (sdh)
Revised 03/02/92 (jen)
Revised 03/31/92 (jen)
JEN:REVISION.92M
Revised 04/29/92 (jen)
Revised 07/28/92 (jen)
Revised 02/24/93 (jen)
JEN:ACADGOAL.293

Mission of Hope College

The mission of Hope College is to offer with recognized excellence, academic programs in liberal arts, in the setting of a residential, undergraduate, coeducational college, and in the context of the Christian faith.

Purpose of Hope College

The purpose of Hope College is to provide comprehensive literary and scientific courses of study, including related research and scholarly pursuits, and to do so in relation to the Christian faith with an overall goal of enabling students to grow and mature intellectually, spiritually, culturally, and socially and to prepare for positions of leadership in the nation and the world.

Qualities Hope College Seeks in its Faculty

A.   Significant academic and professional achievement.

B.   Demonstrated ability or potential as an outstanding teacher.

C.   The desire and ability to continue to advance as a teacher and as a professional through the pursuit of high quality scholarly and/or artistic work, and, if possible, to involve students in such work.

D.   A commitment to:

1. the ideals of liberal education

2. encouraging students to develop a coherent value system for learning and for all of life

3. the historic Christian faith and to fulfilling with excellence the purpose of the college as outlined above.

LIBRARY INFORMATION

NAME TAGS - will be ordered by the secretaries.

REQUESTED FORMS - Below are forms contained in the yellow folder marked "Request Forms" on top of the secretaries' office file cabinet:

-<u>Motor Vehicle Registration</u> for obtaining a campus parking sticker.
-<u>Cash Payment requestions</u> for requesting a check from the Business Office.
    Note: Must be approved and signed by David.
-<u>Inter-departmental charge form</u> is used when charging or crediting another department on campus. Note: Must be signed by David.
-<u>Request for Travel Reimbursement</u> when incurring expenses on a trip. (Green color)
    Note: Must be signed by David.
-<u>Request for Authorization of Payment to a Staff or Faculty Member</u>
-<u>Absence forms</u> to be filled out <u>before</u> a planned absence. Note: Must be approved and signed by David. Is then mailed to the Provost for his signature.
-<u>Work request forms</u> to be filled out when turning work in to the secretaries.

RESEARCH GUIDES - are usually ordered in a large quantity, so when the desk area supplies becomes low, please check for an additional supply. To re-order please notify the secretaries by giving them a sample copy along with the number of copies needed. (Research guides are duplicated in the same color stock.) They will order from the campus Copy Center. It takes a minimum of two days depending on department work load.

STAFF CALENDAR - Please record your planned absences, vacations, etc., as much in advance as possible on the library system.

SUPPLIES - A cabinet of various supplies such as tape, glue sticks, staples, pens, etc. is kept in the secretaries' office. You may help yourself to any of these items but please notify the secretary if the you are taking the last one. Purchasing library and office supplies should be done through the secretaries. Please determine as exactly as possible what is needed using the Geneva Bookstore catalog and give the information to the secretary. Our student couriers will be able to pick up certain supplies on their scheduled runs.

TELEPHONE - When you will be away from your desk for awhile, your phone can be forwarded to another desk in the library or to the staff lounge. Press *3 and then the number to which you want your phone forwarded. To cancel the forward, press #3. Please notify the secretary and your supervisor if you will not be working your usual hours for that day.

WORD PROCESSING - Any copying of documents of 25 or more is done at a cost savings by the college Copy Center. A pink order form is completed and clipped to the orignal. It is then placed in the "Hand Delivery" basket in the library receiving room, to be taken by the courier on her/his scheduled run. Note: Please let the secretaries know when a large request is made in order to work with the courier on pick-up of items. Also, any special rush items should be marked and brought to the courier's/secretaries' attention for special handling.

_____

_____

LIBRARY COLLECTION DEVELOPMENT POLICY

The overall responsibility for the quality of the collection rests upon the library staff. Because no one person is able to have extensive knowledge of the wide range of subjects represented by Hope's curriculum, the classroom faculty is asked, indeed they are encouraged, to participate in the selection of books, journals and other materials for the collection. The role of the librarians is one of coordination and oversight, ensuring that no major areas of the curriculum are without resources, bringing new publications to the attention of interested faculty, and anticipating needs in subjects of developing interest to the college community.

The basic principles upon which we develop the collection were set forth in the document written in 1985 and may be summarized as follows: I. The collection must be developed to support the curriculum first. All other needs such as research, recreation, or entertainment must be subordinate to the requirements of the curriculum. II. The library will build upon its existing strengths, but will maintain all subjects in the curriculum at least at the adequate level.

TECHNICAL SERVICES DEPARTMENTS
NEW STAFF TRAINING

Overview - Who do you see?

___ ___ Acquisitions = Books, bookkeeping, library supplies, gifts, office supplies.

___ ___ Serials = Periodicals, binding, couriers, mail sorting.

___ ___ Cataloging = Cataloging, processing, easy binds, new book lists, database problems, lost or discarded items, items that need recataloging or online modifications.

___ ___ Book repair

___ ___ Standing orders

Acquisitions

___ ___ Demonstration of Data Research Associates

Acquisitions System

___ ___ Procedure for placing book order:

How to fill out cards
Budget choice
Approval

___ ___ How to tell if materials are:

on order
received, not yet cataloged
cataloged, in processing
cataloged, available

___ ___ Explanation of library accounts (2-12150-____)

___ ___ Procedures for departmental orders

___ ___ Demonstration of BIP-CD

Search versus Browse
Searching strategies

Cataloging

__ __   Location of library materials in technical services
Uncataloged books
Uncataloged periodicals/standing orders
Uncataloged audio-visual, music, et al.
Cataloged materials

__ __   Policies regarding material in technical services

Serials

__ __   Demonstration of Data Research Associates Serials System

How to tell:
location and format of titles
holding of each format
status of each issue

How to search for missing journals
Copy of instructions/suggestions

How to find in the receiving room:
volumes with missing issues
damaged books and periodicals
bindery prep material

Overview

__ __   Understanding of OCLC System

__ __   General technical services workflow

CATALOG DEPARTMENT

* Indicates checklist items for all staff; other items are pecifically for new Catalog Department employees.

____ ___ *Function of the Catalog Department

____ ___ *Workflow

____ ___ *Location of files (shelf list)

____ ___ *Catalog/Database

____ ___ *Withdrawals (lost and discarded items)

____ ___ Library of Congress copy cataloging (monographs)

____ ___ OCLC member copy cataloging (monographs)

____ ___ Original cataloging

____ ___ Audio-visual items cataloging (locations)

____ ___ Serials (cataloging, LDR's, serial system)

____ ___ Authority work:

____ ___ Name

____ ___ Series

____ ___ Subject

____ ___ OCLC transfer

____ ___ OCLC change requests

Hope College

*Indicates checklist items for reference staff.

<u>Circulation</u>

_____ _____ LC
_____ _____ Borrower Services
_____ _____ Charge
_____ _____ Discharge
_____ _____ New Card Adjustment
_____ _____ Renewal
_____ _____ Quick Registration
_____ _____ Borrower Status
_____ _____ Borrower Fine List
_____ _____ Borrower Info. Display
_____ _____ Pay Fines
_____ _____ Pay All Fines
_____ _____ On-the-Fly Books
_____ _____ On-the-Fly Files
         ___ ___ Charge of
         ___ ___ Discharge of
_____ _____ Using Screenprints

<u>*Granberg Room</u>

_____ _____ *Showing Videos
_____ _____ *Showing 16mm. Films
_____ _____ *Showing Slides
_____ _____ *Screen
_____ _____ *VT 220 Hookup
_____ _____ *Microcomputer Hookup

<u>*Microform</u>

_____ _____ *Grauls
_____ _____ *How to Find Fiche & Film
_____ _____ *Microfiche r/p
_____ _____ *Microfilm r/p
_____ _____ *Copy Keys or Cards

<u>Curriculum Library</u>

_____ _____ Kits
_____ _____ Books
_____ _____ Files

<u>*IMC</u>

_____ _____ Laminators   _____ _____ 3M
_____ _____ Paper cutters   _____ _____ Primary
_____ _____ Ditto   Typewriter
_____ _____ Thermofax   _____ _____ Opaque Projector

<u>Microcomputers</u> _____ _____   <u>AV Playback</u> _____ _____

116 - Comprehensive Training Documents

CIRCULATION

*Indicates checklist items for reference staff; other items are specifically for new Circulation Department employees.

____ ____ *Library loan periods/fine schedule

____ ____ *Privacy Act

____ ____ *Campus security/building security

____ ____ *Library staff borrowing privileges and procedures

____ ____ *Library usage for non-Hope patrons

____ ____ *Placing building maintenance service calls

____ ____ *Rules for school-age children in the library

____ ____ *Interlibrary loan request pickup

____ ____ *Procedures for library searches

____ ____ *Hold request system for library books

____ ____ *Reserve materials: locating, charging, & discharging

____ ____ *Reserve request forms for faculty

____ ____ *Lost and found

____ ____ Public service philosophy for Circulation

____ ____ Desk shifts

____ ____ Opening procedures

____ ____ Daily circulation procedures

____ ____ Vending machine policy and service calls

____ ____ *3M Detection System

____ ____ *Copy machines

____ ____ Change machine

____ ____ Audit procedures

____ ____ *Checking out materials and overrides/special permission
____ ____ *Checking in materials

____ ____ *Delinquent patron policy & procedure

____ ____ *Book returns

____ ____ *Placing equipment service calls

Hope College

_____ _____ *Issuing library cards

_____ _____ Fine payment procedure

_____ _____ Closing procedure

_____ _____ *Student time cards

_____ _____ *Private faculty carrels

_____ _____ *Circulation manual

_____ _____ *Photocopy loans

_____ _____ *Lost book payment policy & procedure

_____ _____ *Collection arrangement

_____ _____ Call number order teaching for shelf management

_____ _____ Shelf management assignment notebooks

_____ _____ Shelf management and shelf reading procedures

_____ _____ *Sending damaged books to mending

_____ _____ *Relation to WTS Circulation

_____ _____ *Computer controlled lighting system

_____ _____ Circulation policies

REFERENCE

*Indicates checklist items for all staff; other items are specifically for new Reference Department employees.

____ ____ *Ready reference collection

____ ____ *Index tables

____ ____ *Reference stacks

____ ____ *Special collections

    ___ ___ *Vertical file

    ___ ___ *Annual reports

    ___ ___ *Atlas case

____ ____ *Reference staff

____ ____ Bibliographic instruction

____ ____ *Database searching

____ ____ *Collection development

____ ____ *Government documents and census

____ ____ *ILL

    ___ ___ *Service to patrons

    ___ ___ *Service to staff

____ ____ Nuclear Regulatory Commission Documents

____ ____ Public services philosophy for reference

____ ____ Reference interview techniques

____ ____ Opening/closing procedures

____ ____ Reference desk file cabinets

____ ____ Mail distribution; E-mail

Hope College

LIBRARY REFERENCE TECHNOLOGY

___ ___ DRA online training

___ ___ PAC; databases available

___ ___ Keyword Boolean

___ ___ Printers and paper

___ ___ Serials

___ ___ CD/ROM computers

___ ___ SilverPlatter

___ ___ STN

___ ___ Current contents

___ ___ Citation indexes

___ ___ Census

___ ___ Internet

___ ___ Merit

NEW EMPLOYEE ORIENTATION CHECKLIST VERIFICATIONS

Indicate with an X each completed section.

I.   FIRST DAY

_____ Supervisor's initial orientation first day

II. FIRST TWO WEEKS

_____ Orientation common to all departments

_____ Tour of the library

III. FIRST TWO MONTHS

_____ Acquistions & Receiving Department

_____ Catalog Department

_____ Circulation Department

_____ Library Media Center

_____ Overview of Public Services

_____ Overview of Technical Services

_____ Preservation of library materials

_____ Reference Department

_____ Library technology training

_____ Tour of main campus

IV. CONCLUSION OF ORIENTATION PERIOD

_____ Meeting with Director

_____

Employee's Signature   Date

_____

Supervisor's Signature   Date

_____

Director's Signature   Date

SUPERVISOR'S INITIAL ORIENTATION FIRST DAY

I.   FIRST DAY

Welcome!

_____ _____ Introduction

_____ _____ Director

_____ _____ Head of Public Services

_____ _____ Head of Technical Services

___ ___ All other library staff

_____ _____ Hours of work

___ ___ Flexible scheduling

___ ___ Medical appointments

___ ___ Collegiality

___ ___ Breaks

___ ___ Meal times and places

_____ _____ Library general keys

_____ _____ Address form

_____ _____ Name tag

_____ _____ Smoking regulations

_____ _____ Food and Drink regulations

COMMON TO ALL DEPARTMENTS

II. FIRST TWO WEEKS

____ ____ College organizational chart

____ ____ Library organizational chart

____ ____ Emergency procedures

   ___ ___ medical

   ___ ___ crime

   ___ ___ weather

   ___ ___ Public Safety

   ___ ___ Disaster response plan

____ ____ Microcomputers

   ___ ___ locations in other departments

   ___ ___ passwords; VAX account, library accounts

____ ____ Readings (as applies to your position)

   ___ ___ library annual report

   ___ ___ long range goals and objectives

   ___ ___ college mission statement

   ___ ___ departmental policies and procedures manual

   ___ ___ library guide

   ___ ___ library handouts/bibliographies

   ___ ___ collection development policy

   ___ ___ faculty handbook

   ___ ___ librarian evaluation standards

____ ____ Photocopier

   ___ ___ adding paper

   ___ ___ adding toner

   ___ ___ changing paper size

   ___ ___ paper jams

   ___ ___ paper storage

   ___ ___ collating

___ ___ reduce/enlarge

____ ____ Telefax Machine

___ ___ adding paper

___ ___ sending text

___ ___ dialing

____ ____ Library Committees

____ ____ Telephone

___ ___ etiquette

___ ___ transfer/hold

___ ___ call forwarding

___ ___ long distance phone calls

___ ___ access code

____ ____ Tour of Campus

____ ____ Tour of Western Seminary Library

____ ____ Tour of Herrick Public Library

The following four forms are used by the librarian in charge of database searching (samples attached):

    1.   Online Literature Search Request (blue form)

    2.   Database Search Record

    3.   Database Search Cash Deposit/Database Search Charge

    4.   Inter-Departmental Charge Form

1. Online Literature Search Request

This is the form which records the original database search request.

Searches may be requested by Hope College faculty or students or by non-Hope individuals. Faculty and students are charged the cost of the search minus a $7.50 subsidy; non-Hope individuals are charged the cost of the search plus a $25.00 fee.

The Search Request form may be filled out by the requester on his/her own or, when possible, by the librarian who will perform the search in consultation with the requester. When possible an appointment may be made for this purpose.

The information on this form determines the manner in which the searcher will proceed. The form should be completed to whatever degree the librarian feels necessary to enable an efficient search.

Two important numbers are assigned to this original search request form. One is the search number itself. Search numbers are assigned by year, e.g. "91" for the year 1991, and then by the number of searches done in a given year. For example, the first search performed in 1991 was numbered "1" and recorded as "91-1."

The other number first recorded here is the Interdepartmental Acct. No. This is the number of the college account to be billed for search costs and should be obtained from the faculty member and/or student requesting the search if they wish to bill the search to a college account.

This form is filed in the Blue Database Notebook.

2. Database Search Record

This form is completed after a database search has been made. It is the record of that particular search and should include the Search No. assigned, the number of the account to be billed (if any), patron information, and dates.

The "charges" section should record minimally "database(s) searched," "time online," and "total cost."

After recording the total cost for all databases searched, any credit should be noted ($7.50 subsidy for faculty and students) and/or any extra charges noted ($25.00 charge for non-Hope searches). The final "total charge" should be computed here and this amount will be transferred to Forms 3 and 4.

This form is filed in front of the Online Literature Search Request form in the Blue Database Notebook.

3. Database Search Cash Deposit/Database Search Charge

This form is used for both cash deposits (as it states) and to record amounts charged to other college accounts.

In the first case (Form 3, A), if a search cost is paid in cash or by check, this form is filled out to accompany the check or cash. It is given to the Library Accounts Person (currently Dawn).

The same form (somewhat altered; see Form 3, B) is also used to record that a charge is to be made to some other college account. In place of "Deposit" write "Charge" and enter the amount of the charge. Also enter the Account No. to be charged. Again the form is given to Library Accounts.

4. Inter-Departmental Charge Form

This form is used only when another college account is being billed for a database search.

The completed form must include the Department Name and Account No. to be billed. It also includes the date, the amount to be billed, and the Search No.

When completed, this form is given to the Library Director. The Director will sign the form and forward it to the appropriate department.

THE INTERLIBRARY LOAN OFFICE

Become familiar with the following items in the Interlibrary Loan Office:

_____ Materials that Hope has **borrowed** from other schools
This includes:
- the wooden bookshelf where books that have been received are kept, but have not been transferred to Circulation because the patron has not been contacted.
- a master computer printout of current OCLC transactions for Hope patrons.
- a rolodex of Hope Lenders (schools that lend to Hope).
- the ILL mail book which helps us keep track of the dates books were mailed back to the school that lent them to us.
- the paper file of all ILL transactions active on OCLC, all but the lower left hand file have to do with borrowing.

_____ Materials that Hope has **lent** to other schools
This includes:
- the lower left hand corner of the brown file cabinet.
- the blue overdue basket.
- the ILL mail book which helps us keep track of the dates which boks were mailed to the borrowing library.
- a rolodex of Hope borrowers (schools that borrow from Hope).

_____ Interlibrary Loan Supplies
This includes:
- Jiffy Bags
- large and small manila envelopes
- Hope College envelopes, stationery, and mailing labels
- additional blue and white ILL request cards
- cleaning supplies

_____ Books and Indexes needed in Interlibrary Loan
This includes:
- The <u>American Library Directory</u>
- Copyright Compliance catalogs
- <u>CASSI</u>
- an older copy of <u>The Serials Directory</u>
- the OCLC manual for Interlibrary Loan
- OCLC catalogs arranged by OCLC symbol (blue) and institution name (green)

_____ Miscellaneous Interlibrary Loan Materials
This includes:
- the mail bin for campus, van, and outgoing mail.
- the ILL job manual describing the aspects of both lending and borrowing.
- a VAX manual including VT220 directions, MIRLYN directions, and some library system directions.

Hope College

DATE: July 19, 1993

TO: All Faculty

FROM: David Jensen
            Kelly Jacobsma

RE: Copyright Permission for Library Reserve Material

Since the 1976 Copyright Law went into effect, the library and the college have taken steps to insure that we act in accordance with that law. We pay copyright royalties for materials obtained through Interlibrary Loan and when photocopying materials for course packets. It is clear that we also must adhere to the rules regarding copyright for materials that faculty place on reserve at the library.

Essentially, the rules regarding photocopying material to put on library reserve are similar to those governing multiple copying for use in the classroom. Guidelines outlining such use are enclosed for your information.

We are keenly aware of the burden that would be placed on faculty if we required individual faculty to obtain copyright permission for each item placed on reserve; therefore the library will handle securing copyright permission or paying necessary royalties through the Copyright Clearance Center's Transactional Reporting Service. Adhering to these guidelines will of course necessitate that we make some changes in how material is placed on reserve. We will need a complete citation for each photocopied item that is to be placed on reserve. The complete citation should be either written on or attached to the photocopied item.

We will also need to know if you intend to place the item on reserve for one semester only or if this item will be placed on reserve in subsequent semesters. **If a photocopy is used in multiple courses or in successive years, copyright permission must be obtained, even if only one copy of the work is placed on reserve.**

Enclosed you will find the copyright guidelines as they apply to reserve material and a packet with updated forms and instructions for placing material on reserve. If we can assist you in preparing your course materials to be placed on reserve please contact Joyce Nielsen at 7889.

SHELF MANAGEMENT AND MENDING PROCEDURES   7/13/93

1.   Damaged items found by shelf management students when
     shelving in stacks or found by circulation students when
     discharging items or loading carts, should be placed on the
     "Damaged Item" shelf.

2.   The shelf management team will change the item status to
     "damaged" and the location code to "technical services"
     (99). Books are then placed on the "to be mended shelf".

3.   Students from mending will come and retrieve books from the
     "to be mended shelf" as space in the mending area becomes
     available.

     NOTE: Journals should not be placed on the to be mended
     shelf but taken directly to the mending staff or given to
     Pat.

4.   As soon as books are repaired and processed, the mending
     staff will put them on the "return from mending shelf".(The
     status and location will have been changed by technical
     services during processing.)

5.   The shelf management staff will check the "return from
     mending shelf" daily. Items will be checked for the
     following: * tattle tape in place and working
                 * spine label right-side up and readable
                 * call number visible and secure
                 * status has been changed to available
                 * location information has been changed

ITEMS IN PROCESS PROCEDURES

1.   If an item says **In Process**, print the screen, put the
      patrons name on it and give to technical services. A hold
      should also be put on the book at the circulation desk.

2.   If an item does not say in process there is currently no way
      to know if the item is in the building. Place a hold on the
      book at the circulation so that the patron will be notified
      when the book is available.

LIBRARY COLLECTION DEVELOPMENT POLICY

The overall responsibility for the quality of the collection rests upon the library staff. Because no one person is able to have extensive knowledge of the wide range of subjects represented by Hope's curriculum, the classroom faculty is asked, indeed they are encouraged, to participate in the selection of books, journals and other materials for the collection. The role of the librarians is one of coordination and oversight, ensuring that no major areas of the curriculum are without resources, bringing new publications to the attention of interested faculty, and anticipating needs in subjects of developing interest to the college community.

The basic principles upon which we develop the collection were set forth in the document written in 1985 and may be summarized as follows: I. The collection must be developed to support the curriculum first. All other needs such as research, recreation, or entertainment must be subordinate to the requirements of the curriculum. II. The library will build upon its existing strengths, but will maintain all subjects in the curriculum at least at the adequate level.

INTERLIBRARY LOAN AT THE REFERENCE DESK

Handing Out the Form

When handing out an Interlibrary Loan form, describe the sections of the form to the patron, and explain the following:

1. The patron should check our Public Access System (PAC) to make sure the material is not in our collection.

2. The patron should realize that a seperate form is needed for **each** book or magazine article that they are requesting.

3. Emphasize to the patron how important it is to fill out the top of the request form with the correct information about the author or title of a book or about the Periodical title, author and article title, plus volume number, date and pages the article appears on.

4. Every form needs a patron signature, address and telephone number.

5. Every form turned in by a student **must** have a faculty signature.

6. The Interlibrary Loan process usually takes about 1-2 weeks but may take longer. If the patron has a deadline to meet they should indicate that on the form in the Date no Longer Needed space.

7. If the patron knows that the material is owned at Hope but at the bindery or missing, please indicate this on the form in the Remarks section.

Taking the Form

When the Interlibrary Loan request is submitted at the Reference Desk, carefully examine it while the patron is **still** at the desk. Check for missing or incorrect information and the following:

1. Is the information filled out completely?

2. Is the serial information recorded at the right place. Does it include Vol., date, and pages, etc.?

3. Is the form signed by both the patron and a faculty member?

4. Is the handwriting legible?

The request is then placed in the plastic basket behind the Reference Desk to be picked up by Interlibrary Loan. Remember to tell the patron that he/she will be notified by telephone or campus mail when a book comes in, which may then be picked up at the Circulation Desk. Photocopies will be mailed directly to the

patron unless other arrangements are made. Books should be
returned to either of the main circulation desks, dropped in the
overnight slot, or returned directly to the ILL office.
Telephone requests for Interlibrary Loan materials should be
referrred to the ILL office (x7794).

Interlibrary Loan Renewals

One renewal request will be submitted on borrowed materials
unless the lending library states a policy of no renewals. The
request must be made to the ILL office **before** the borrowed
material becomes overdue. When a patron requests a renewal, note
the ILL transaction number, patron name, and title of the book.
Give this information to the ILL office. Remind the patron to
check with the ILL office in a few days to see if the renewal was
accepted and to get the new due date.

```
                    VAN WYLEN LIBRARY
                    GRANBERG ROOM POLICY
```

During the academic year, the primary use of the Van Wylen Library Granberg Room is as a classroom for library instruction and for college related use of audio visual materials. Due to heavy demand for this room, advanced booking is required.

The Granberg Room has a seating capacity of 38. When tables are used, seating is limited to 27. The room contains a lectern and overhead projector. AV equipment in the projection room includes a 16mm motion picture projector, 1/2" and 3/4" video recording/projection equipment, slide projector with remote control, audio cassette player, and a video projector with cabling that allows projection of a DEC VT 220 terminal and Apple microcomputer. Media Services Desk personnel will set up and run projection equipment in the control room. Reservations must be made in advance for this service.

Only light food service, such as coffee and rolls, will be permitted in the Granberg Room. Food arrangements must be made with Food Service.

To reserve the Granberg Room and make arrangements for services, please contact the library secretary at 7790.

HOPE COLLEGE LIBRARIES
GIFT POLICY

Gifts to a college library can be a source of collection enrichment. Specific gifts often enable a library to achieve excellence in an area where it might not otherwise excel. For this reason gifts and their donors are much appreciated by the Library and the College. However, it is recognized that gifts/donations are not without cost to the library. As a rule, the addition of gifts to the collection are made on the same basis as purchased materials. The time it takes to process gift items (check, catalog, and prepare for circulation) can be problematic for the library. Accordingly, the following guidelines/policies have been adopted by the Hope College Libraries regarding gifts.

MONETARY GIFTS

Monetary gifts to the Library should be made through the College's Development Office and designated for the Library. As a rule monetary gifts are unrestricted and are used to purchase materials falling within the Collection Development Policy of the Library.   Monetary gifts for specific or designated purchases must be approved by the Director of the Libraries prior to acceptance. This is to ensure that the materials purchased fit within the guidelines of the Collection Development Policy.

BOOK/MONOGRAPH GIFTS

The acceptance of specific book or monograph gifts is dependent upon an examination (either by list of titles or by physical examination) to ensure that the material is relevant to the needs and/or goals of the Library and fit within the parameters of the Collection Development Policy. In addition, factors like date, edition, and condition of the books/monographs are also considered before acceptance of the material.

GIFTS OF SERIALS

Gift subscriptions of serials (journals, newspapers, magazines) are encouraged. However, such gifts require some special handling. Unlike a gift of a book or monograph, the gift of a periodical subscription entails a commitment by either the donor or the library. Incomplete serial runs are of limited value to the library. The availability of indexing, the format of the subscription and/or the cost of binding and storage are additional factors to be considered in serial gift subscriptions. It is recommended that donors of serials consult first with the Director of the Libraries regarding their gift.   Unsolicited and unannounced subscriptions arriving at the Library are treated as "sample" issues.

VAN WYLEN LIBRARY

PUBLIC NOTICE DISPLAY POLICY

There are six public bulletin boards: one in the student lounge and one in each of the five copier rooms. (All other bulletin boards are staff bulletin boards; their contents are to be determined solely by the staff in charge of the area.)

The public bulletin boards provide limited space for students to post announcements of activities and notices, such as books for sale or roommates needed. We do not display partisan politican literature or commercially prepared information such as ads for foreign travel, magazines, graduate school, credit cards, etc. Written or graphic material that is intended to be derogatory of a racial or ethnic group will not be posted.

STUDENT NOTICES
* Must be tacked on a public bulletin board
* Must be dated
* Must be no larger than 11" by 17"
* No more than one notice per board for each activity
    Items meeting these requirements are left up until the date of activity but no more than one month.

COLLEGE EVENTS AND PERFORMANCES
These events are advertised in many places, so their notices are displayed in the library for only a short time, if at all. Special events may be advertised on the easel. (Decisions on display will be made by library staff.)

PUBLICATIONS
Such publications as the Anchor, Inklings, Opus, etc., are displayed for distribution in bins on the oak counter in front of the bulletin board in the student lounge.

Items found displayed elsewhere in Van Wylen do not meet these guidelines and will be removed by the library staff.

These guidelines will be sent to Student Government and to each of the student organizations, including fraternities and sororities.

HOW TO REQUEST AN ITEM WHICH IS NOT YET CATALOGED

1. Make a printout of the basic title screen.
2. Make sure patron **has** a library card.
3. Write your name on the printout.
4. Write patron's full name and phone number on the printout.

5. Take the printout to circulation and have them put a hold on the title for the patron.
6. Tell the patron that we will make every effort to contact them when the item has been put on the hold shelf OR they are welcome to check back themselves by calling circulation after at least one full working day has passed.

7. Then take the printout to a member of the technical services staff who handles books. (Nancy, Chris, Colleen, Dawn, or Gloria)
8. If there is absolutely no one in technical services, put the printout in the mail box of a technical services staff person. If necessary, check the staff calendar to make sure they are going to be working.

9. If in house, the item will be processed and sent to the hold shelf as soon as possible.
10. If the item is not in house, the patron will be so notified.

Interlibrary Loan FAX Policy
Van Wylen Library
Hope College

The FAX machine located in the Van Wylen Library Reference office is intended for use by the Interlibrary Loan, Library, and Archives staff only. Students and faculty of Hope College are requested to use the FAX machines located in the Word Processing office on the second floor of DeWitt. FAX machines are available for non-Hope patrons at several commercial establishments. (See Reference Rolodex)

Outgoing FAX requests for Hope Interlibrary Loan patrons are limited to rush requests approved by a librarian.

Standard Interlibrary Loan procedures are to be followed for FAX requests and should comply to copyright restrictions. Standard ALA or OCLC workforms should be used. All requests are to include bibliographic information and verification. When verification is not provided this should be indicated.

FAX phone number, contact person, and phone number of the contact person should be included on the request form. Requested return delivery time should be indicated. (One week, 2 working days, 24 hours, or 3 hours) Same day return requires a phone call to the lending library. Books must be delivered by mail or van delivery.

Requesting library should use a cover sheet including organization name and contact person.

When filling an Interlibrary Loan by FAX, the article, the request form and a cover sheet should be included. The maximum number of pages per FAX request is not to exceed 15. Unfilled requests require an unfilled request form to be sent back to the requesting library.

FAX phone number and directions are posted on the FAX machine table.

Interlibrary Loan Department Policy
Van Wylen Library
Hope College

Interlibrary Loan (ILL) is a library service provided for Hope College faculty, staff and students. Materials not owned by Hope College libraries are obtained from other lending libraries. The cost of these items is absorbed by Hope College. All student requests are required to include a faculty signature.

Local businesses who have set up an ILL account may use Interlibrary Loan by paying a $5.00 service charge per item ordered plus any fees charged by the lending library. The library does not provide Interlibrary Loan for non-Hope users except with special permission by a librarian and at the above fees.

Request forms may be obtained at the Van Wylen Library Reference desk or from the Interlibrary Loan office. White request forms are for books and blue forms are for photocopies. Faculty and staff requests will also be accepted on the VAX (account is EINBERGERH). Phone requests will be honored for faculty or staff when necessary. Completed Interlibrary Loan request forms may be placed in the basket behind the Reference desk, mailed, or turned in to the Interlibrary Loan office.

A one to two week waiting period is needed to obtain Interlibrary Loan requests. Rush requests may be obtained by telefax. (See FAX policy.) Items owned by Hope but in use or at the bindery are requested through Interlibrary Loan with special permission only.

Photocopies are mailed out to patrons as soon as they have been marked received by the Interlibrary Loan office. They are mailed through campus mail or first class mail. Books are processed in the Interlibrary Loan office, a sleeve of Interlibrary Loan information is attached and a phone call or message is sent to the patron. Once the patron is notified, the book is placed on the Interlibrary Loan shelf at the Main Circulation Desk in Van Wylen for the patron to pick up. The patron is required to sign for any requests picked up in this manner. Photocopies need not be returned. Books and other materials should be returned by the due date listed on the Interlibrary Loan sleeve. There is a limit of one renewal request per item. Permission for renewal is at the discretion of the lending library. Books and similar materials may not be borrowed for the purpose of putting on reserve.

Materials may be returned at any Hope College Libraries Circulation desk or at the Interlibrary Loan office. Any overdue fines or charges resulting from the failure to return materials are the responsibility of the patron--not Hope College.

GROUP STUDY USE POLICY

1. Group studies are intended for the use of Hope College students studying together.

2. Two or more people constitute a group.

3. Groups have priority over individual users. Therefore groups may ask individual students to leave a study so that the group may use the room. Groups should not displace individuals if other group studies are available. Larger groups may NOT displace smaller groups.

4. Individual students may use a group study when it is not requested by a group.

5. Groups not affiliated with the college may NOT displace Hope College students from group studies. But, see exception below.

6. From time to time group studies may be used for special purposes such as Model UN, Young Authors Conference, seminars, or converted temporarily to private studies.

7. Group studies may be reserved for the use of groups studying together. Call the library secretary at 7790 to reserve a study. Reservations will be accepted for study groups, but not for committee meetings.

D R A F T

VAN WYLEN LIBRARY DISABILITY RESOURCE ROOM
GUIDELINES

1. Individuals will be permitted access to this room by:

    A. Receiving approval through the Director of Disabled
        Student Services;

    B. Following participation in training provided by CIT
        staff.

2. Individuals will receive access to this room by presenting
    their campus identification card (student, staff or faculty)
    to the attendants at the second floor Media Services Desk.
    They will be expected to leave their ID in exchange for the
    key to the resource room.

3. Students will be permitted to bring one person in this room
    with them. This could be a study partner, a tutor, a test
    proctor, a reader or a Hope faculty or staff member.

4. Any requests for use of this room for demonstration purposes
    or group gatherings must be made to the Director of
    Libraries.

5. Working dogs must be fed or watered in the library rest
    rooms or other buildings on campus.

6. Individuals who have problems with the equipment should
    direct inquiries to CIT, X7670.

7. This room is for the use of Hope students, faculty and
    staff. Exceptions will be made after consultation with the
    Director of Disabled Student Services and the Director of
    Libraries.

REFERENCE DEPARTMENT ORIENTATION

INTRODUCTION AND DISTRIBUTION TRAINING MATERIALS

A. General material

    1. Training schedule

    2. Campus Map

    3. Library Mission Statement

    4. Library Organization Chart

    5. Collection Development Policy

    6. Reference FACETS, Library floor plan, diagram of Reference shelves

    7. Reference Forms: statistics, incident reports, public services monthly activities, information for the calendar, request for satellite campuses, request for library instruction, interlibrary loan

    8. Reference Area Protocol

    9. Katz, W. "The Reference Interview." Introduction to Reference Work, vol. II.

B. DIALOG

C. CD - ROMS

D. Lexis/Westlaw

E. FirstSearch

F. Internet

MODULE I. OBJECTIVE: To provide an understanding of the physical plant, administrative arrangement, and services of the library departments.

    A.   Introduction

        1.   Review   of   Library   floor   plan

        2.   Special collections

           a) Curriculum Lab and childrens

           b) Boldt

           c) Hoyt

           d) ERIC documents

           e) Annual Reports

        3. Satellites

           a) Ballston

           b) Loudoun

    B.   Tour and Introduction to Other Staff Members and Functions

        1. Public Services

           a) Layout: CircDesk, In/Out board, mail boxes, keys, staff area, supply cabinet, pc, DocDirect printer, vendacard dispenser, Reference bulletin board, librarian offices, staff computer, photocopier and fax.

           b) Reference functions: reference desk inquiries, telephone service, instruction in ALADIN and databases, CD-ROMs, LEXIS and Internet use, computer searching, inputting interlibrary loans, library instruction, publications

c) Circulation functions: book check in/out, reserves, consortia arrangements, telephone, photocopy vendacards, photocopy, DocDirect copies

d) Application for photocopy code and Internet address

2. Serials/Acquisitions/Cataloging/ Interlibrary loan

3. Library public areas

   a) four floors

   b) entrance/exit

   c) faculty study

   d) student study rooms

   e) special collections

4. Reinsch Building

   a) IMC

   b) LRC

   c) handicapped bathroom

   d) exits

   e) auditorium

MODULE II. OBJECTIVES: To understand public services and methods/procedures of providing those services.

   A. Review of Reference Area Protocol

   B. Reference Desk

1.   desk etiquette: wear your nametag, don't leave without a substitute, coverage schedule see Bulletin Board, absence - call Jean Tolbert before 7:30am at 703 - 892 - 3453

2.   ALADIN: databases, training mode, staff mode, Telnet

3.   TODAY clipboard

4.   name plates

5.   miscellaneous supplies

6.   calendar

7.   journal holdings lists

8.   Reference Manual

9.   microfiche reader

10.   ADA log

C.   Reference area

    1.   ready reference collection

    2.   dictionary

    3.   map collection

    4.   material for distribution

    5.   exhibit case

    6.   facets kiosk

    7.   public ALADIN

    8.   LAN, other workstations

    9.   Reference Department Shelves

D.   The Reference Interview

    1.   information vs instruction

    2.   communication: courtesy, patience, approachability,

listening

3. identifying the information need

4. referring to another librarian/staff member

5. limits of service: MU vs. consortia members, vs.

outsiders, time pressure

E. Telephone reference

1. mechanics of answering call

2. placing it on hold

3. transferring calls

4. messages

F. Library Instruction

1. refer to LI librarian

2. appointments

3. Form: Request for Library Instruction

G. Computer Searching

1. refer faculty requests (non emergency) and all forms

to librarian responsible for computer searching

2. selling discs

H. Opening/Closing procedure

I. Liaison program

MODULE III. OBJECTIVE: To determine the availability of material,

and its location in Reinsch Library.

A. Physical Arrangement of Collection: book locations,

journal locations, pamphlet file, computer services,

online catalog, closed reserve, reserve

B. books

   1. CATS (see FACETS): record elements, searching by author, title, keyword, subject,

   2. setting the catalog to Marymount holdings

   3. printing: (see FACETS): paper, re-inking, replacing cartridges, other printer problems

   4. reserve material: switching to technical processes mode, reviewing the record

   5. order status: check only for MU faculty/students/staff, offer to notify patron only if book has been received

   6. When ALADIN is down: call technical services or WRLC, put out public notices, use the LC classification scheme

C. journals

   1. CATS records

   2. Reinsch Periodical, Index and Newspaper, Holdings list

   3. Full text serials holdings list

D. ALADIN databases: GENL, PAST, ABII, EDLI, ERIC, REVU, CBIE,

   1. description (see FACETS)

   2. policies

   3. printed aids and online tutorials

   4. dealing with problems

   5. scheduled training sessions

  E. Non-ALADIN databases: Psych, CINAHL, MLA Bibliography, Ethnic Newswatch, DIALOG, FirstSearch, LEXIS/NEXIS

   1. description (see FACETS)

   2. policies

   3. printed aids and online tutorials

   4. dealing with problems

   5. scheduled training sessions

 F. Internet

   1. scheduled training sessions

MODULE IV. OBJECTIVE: To become familiar with the WRLC consortium.

 A. holdings

 B. Consortium Handbook

 C. direct borrowing privileges

 D. storage facility

 E. FACETS

MODULE V. OBJECTIVE: To become familiar with the interlibrary loan service.

 A. policy review

 B. FirstSearch protocol

MODULE VI. OBJECTIVE: To assist library users in use of the library equipment.

 A. Photocopy machines: limits of service, coin operation, vendacard operations, school vendacards, location of public machines, location staff machine (id required)

B. Microform readers

C. Printers

MODULE VII. OBJECTIVE: TO PREPARE FOR EMERGENCIES BY REVIEWING THE

<u>DISASTER MANUAL</u>

MODULE VIII. OBJECTIVE: To substitute at Circulation Desk as required. TRAINING WITH HEAD OF CIRCULATION.

MODULE VIII. (OPTIONAL) OBJECTIVE: To serve the users at the Ballston Campus library.

A. Scope

B. Visit to Ballston

C. Intralibrary transactions

MODULE VIII. OBJECTIVE: To reinforce the material covered above with sample questions.

A. Do we have ... a book?

B. Do we have a book on ...?

C. Do we have a periodical by the name of ...?

D. Why can't I find this magazine downstairs?

E.   Do we have an article on...?

F.   Do we have... a class assignment?

G.   Do you have the book...that the computer says is not charged out?

H.   Where is the bathroom/ xerox/ telephone/ LRC?

I.   The computer is dark, isn't it working?

J.   Where is there a quiet place to study?

K.   Can I use your computer to...?

L.   I'm a student at .../visitor and I've never been here before. How do I take out a book?

M.   I need a DISCLOSURE search.

N.   Where is there information on a business? In Virginia?

O.   What's the APA style Manual?

P.   Is the library open on...?

AND ANOTHER THING...THE ADMINISTRATIVE ASSISTANT OR TRAINER SHOULD HAVE ARRANGED

A.   for the IMC to take an id picture for the Library In/Out Board

B.   for you to have keys to your office and the Library master

C.   for you to get a photcopy code

D.   for you to get an e-mail address

E.   for an order for your desk name plate and name tag

PLEASE CONSULT A COLLEAGUE IF YOU HAVE ANY PROBLEMS

APPENDIX C

MISSION STATEMENT

Reinsch Library
Mission Statement

General

Reinsch Library provides resources and services for the members of the Marymount University community in order to support and enhance the University's curriculum and faculty research. The library staff helps users develop skills needed to effectively use library and information resources and services.

Environment

The library provides an atmosphere that promotes study, encourages scholarly pursuits, and fosters academic excellence that is the primary goal of the University. The Library staff and administration endeavor to provide:

1) an environment which is pleasant, inviting, and conducive to studying and reading.

2) operating hours which are sufficient to realistically accommodate study and faculty requirements.

3) sufficient seating and study areas.

4) a collection which is in usable physical condition and the materials are accessible to the users.

Users

Reinsch Library's resources and services are available to Marymount students, faculty, staff, and administrators. Direct borrowing privileges are also available to individuals who can identify themselves as members of the Washington Library Consortium or the Consortium for Continuing Higher Education in Northern Virginia. Special borrowing privileges can be arranged by individuals not in the above categories at the discretion of the Dean of Library and Learning Services. The in-house use of materials is open to all.

Information Services

Reinsch Library arranges library materials in open stacks in order to provide maximum accessibility to the collection. The ordering, classifying, cataloging, and processing of materials are handled in a timely manner, with the goal of enhancing the user's ability to access the collection. Circulation policies and procedures are established and publicized and designed to provide for both the reasonable use of materials by an individual and the availability of these materials to other potential users. Materials needed for a specific course are maintained in a limited access reserve collection on a semester-to-semester basis.

Reference librarians assist users in making appropriate and effective use of library resources, facilities, and services. Reference assistance is provided by using traditional library materials as well as by accessing automated databases and indexes. Library research is provided through the use of standard reference sources and information retrieval services which facilitate access to resources. Librarians assist users on a one-to-one basis, give group orientations and tours, and provide bibliographic instruction to classes. In addition, the Public Services Department staff produces general information brochures, bibliographies, guides to groups of sources, and hand-outs on specific resources and services to complement staff services.

Library services to the Marymount community are evaluated through questionnaires, an informal poll of library patrons, and library staff assessment of use and service. The library staff continually investigates opportunities to increase services and access to collections beyond the University through cooperative programs with other libraries and library organizations.

Collection

The librarians, in consultation with the faculty, select materials, regardless of format, for the collection which support instruction, student projects, faculty research, and appropriate general informational needs. Policies of selection reflect the current state of knowledge in relevant disciplines and reflect various points of view. The Library's Acquisitions Policy Manual provides guidelines for selection and evaluation of the collection.

The library collection is organized in such a way as to facilitate accessibility and use. Separate collections are developed as needed. Conformance with Library of Congress cataloging is maintained in order to promote cooperation and consistency with other libraries.

Staff

The Library staff consists of qualified librarians and skilled support personnel who can assist users in making appropriate and effective use of library collections, resources, facilities, and services. The overall staff, including students, is of sufficient size and skills to assure the proper functioning of all departments. The staff interacts with faculty and students in promoting the use of library resources and services.

When recruiting staff or determining staff development, a diversity of educational backgrounds and subject specialties is taken into consideration. Staff members should have other abilities besides bibliographic and library skills. The ability to teach on a one-to-one basis is important for all who interact with students. The staff has empathy for users and a concern for their needs so that they are made to feel comfortable in the library and are encouraged to ask for assistance.

Study Facilities

The physical lay-out of the Library reflects the best utilization of the building and its resources and services. Physical space is maintained where individuals and small groups can comfortably engage in learning activities. Every effort is made to maintain an atmosphere of quiet informality which is conducive to effective study and research.

Development

With adequate budget and other financial and administrative support, Reinsch Library seeks to establish and maintain appropriate standards for academic library service. The business of the Library is managed efficiently, according to established principles of library management and in accordance with Marymount policies and practices. The staff maintains a close and meaningful working relationship with administrative and academic departments, academic planning groups, and other user communities to assure effective development of library services consistent with the objectives and programs of the University and to advise the University as to requirements and costs of resources.

Reinsch Library participates in and contributes to local, state, regional, and national library activities. The Reinsch Library staff continues to appraise the Library's ability and responsibility to serve others beyond the Marymount community.

GENERAL REFERENCE SERVICE GUIDELINES AND POLICIES
BOATWRIGHT MEMORIAL LIBRARY
ADOPTED 10/1/89
REVISED 10/91

PURPOSE:

The primary purpose of these guidelines is to propose standards of service for all reference desk staff. The guidelines will help guide current reference staff as well as orient new staff. These guidelines should be useful when policy questions arise or when patrons may wish to see written verification. In addition, the quality of service offered at the desk can be better evaluated against written expectations and standards, and continuity and consistency in the services offered by all desk staff can be achieved. The contents of the manual will be reviewed annually by the Coordinator of Reference Services and Director of Public Services for currency, accuracy, and completeness. Individual changes will be made as the need for them arises.

SERVICES OFFERED BY THE REFERENCE DEPARTMENT

A. General reference questions
B. Location and directional questions
C. Research questions
D. Instructional questions
E. Telephone reference questions
F. Electronic retrieval searches
G. Individual research consultations
H. Group library orientation and instruction
I. Compilation of bibliographies and library guides
J. Assistance in ordering library materials or interlibrary loan materials
K. Collection Management/Development; Liaison Program
L. Retrieval of Rare Books/Special Collections materials
M. Referral to other libraries or organizations in the Richmond area.

LIBRARY USERS

Reference assistance is available to all students, faculty, and staff of the UR community. All other persons, however, are eligible to use UR libraries' resources, as appropriate and as stated below. During extremely busy times, UR patrons receive first priority. Use professional discretion in deciding priorities. General reference staff are not responsible for staffing other service areas and must consider time and other immediate patron needs before leaving the General Reference area.

Non-UR Users:

Members of the community are eligible to use library materials and reference services. Non-UR or special users may also apply for borrowing privileges according to the special borrowers' policy. Special users may also request a computer search and pay the full cost of the search.

All special users have access to government documents. Borrowing privileges may be granted once the patron has submitted a special borrowing application.

High School students are welcome under the High School guidelines (adopted September 1988). High school students who are disruptive or need extensive help should be reported to the Director of Public Services.

RALC Users:

The Richmond Academic Library Consortium is an organization in the Richmond Area whose purpose is to further the development of member libraries. Members include universities, colleges and community colleges and the Virginia State Library.

Ralc users are welcome and are eligible for reference service.

REFERENCE ETHICS

It is necessary to maintain the integrity of both patron and librarian in every transaction. Some general guidelines for ethical consideration are:

- A.   Every patron and library employee is dealt with courteously
- B.   Personal bias is never reflected in services provided
- C.   Each and every patron is treated seriously and with respect for his/her privacy
- D.   Interpretation of information and/orpersonal opinion is not offered. Medical or legal advice or interpretation is never offered
- E.   Sources of information are provided for all information given.

GENERAL SERVICE GUIDELINES

A. BEHAVIOR AND ATTITUDE

Users need to be educated to the fact that individual assistance is the primary responsibility of staff on desk duty, that reference staff are interested in the problems that face library users and are willing to help. Since the attitude and behavior of staff on duty go a long way toward creating an image of the Reference Department, Reference staff should strive to make that image a positive one.

1. **Approachability**

    * make sure patrons know you can be approached with questions
    * acknowledge patrons immediately
    * adopt the attitude that no question and no patron is stupid
    * use tact and empathy in questioning a patron who may need encouragement in requesting help
    * be patient
    * when not giving service, spot and assist patrons seemingly lost or obviously confused or in doubt in the reference area
    * lengthy social conversations either with patrons or colleagues should be avoided
    * when a question takes the staff member away from the desk for more than a few minutes, alert another available staff member to watch the desk and the telephone.

2. **Mobility**

    * be ready to get up and help a patron at an index table or in the reference stacks; pointing may not always get a person to the right place
    * be sure the patron knows how to use the source.

3. **Colleague consideration**

    * in dealing with patrons be respectful of service previously rendered by your colleagues
    * stick to the desk schedule and be on time. Do not leave the desk until another reference librarian has relieved you.
    * remember that when you're scheduled to be on the desk, be there (not in your office or elsewhere)
    * reshelve desk items upon leaving and leave the desk with an organized image.

B.   <u>HANDLING GENERAL INQUIRIES AND LEVELS OF SERVICE</u>

Encourage users to return for further information. This should be an automatic comment made to all patrons each time they are assisted. If possible, return to patrons assisted earlier to inquire if they need further assistance.

Students who need extensive assistance should consider applying for a research consultation. Reference staff should also offer services outside UR, such as interlibrary loan, Center for Research Libraries and database searches.

Learn from all reference colleagues. Do not hesitate to consult with one another.

Show each patron the utmost courtesy and give topnotch service no matter what the level or type of question. Answering questions involves professional image and attitude, empathy, interpersonal skills and interviewing techniques.

Length of time with patrons is always a difficult decision. Consideration should include how busy it is, the number of other patrons waiting for assistance, number of library personnel available to help patrons and the nature of the user's request. If possible, never leave other patrons waiting for lengthy time periods. Get users started on their projects and then return to them as time permits. Some users may need to be referred to the appropriate librarian liaison for further assistance.

Reference interview skills are important. Patrons frequently do not ask for what they actually need. Remember that the simple question, "Where are the encyclopedias?" could mean that it is the only source a student knows to ask for. Find out as much about the patron's topic as possible and offer further assistance. Direct the search to the best possible sources.

C.   TAKING STATISTICS

The purpose of statistics is to assist the department with justifications for additional staff; to decide on service hours for the Reference Department; to supply needed information for Boatwright monthly and annual statistics; and to respond to surveys.

Directional and reference questions are recorded each hour the desk is staffed.

DEFINITIONS FOR REFERENCE AND DIRECTIONAL QUESTIONS

A **reference** transaction consists of an information contact which involves the knowledge, use, recommendations, interpretation or instruction in the use of one or more information sources. Examples of information sources include printed and nonprinted materials, databases, catalogs and other holdings, records and archives as well as communication and/or referral to other libraries, institutions and individuals. If a transaction includes both a directional and reference question, record the transaction as one reference question. If the same source is used consecutively with different individuals, record a reference question for each library user.

> EXAMPLES: What is the office address of Governor Baliles?
> How long is the James River?
> Where can I find information on sexism in the college classroom?
> Where can I locate *Consumer Reports*?
> How do I use the *New York Times Index*?
> What do these numbers mean in the Serials Holdings List?

A **directional** transaction is an information contact that does not involve the knowledge, use, recommendations, interpretation or instruction in the use of information sources. For example, a directional question deals with information about locations, schedules (such as library hours), floor plans, handbooks or policies, giving instruction in locating staff, library users, or physical features and giving assistance of a non-bibliographic nature with machines.

> **EXAMPLES:** Is this the library?
> Where is the LRC?
> How do I work the copy machine?
> Where do I find the PN's?

Paraphrased from: American Library Association. Library Data Collection Handbook. February, 1981.

D.   TELEPHONE USE

Answer each call in a courteous manner, giving your name and the name of the department. **Example:** "Boatwright Reference, this is John Doe".

Priority goes to in-person users. Telephone inquiries may have to be called back when time allows. Staff should check the Audix message file at least every hour when they are on desk duty and when they leave the desk.

Catalog check -- check holdings status for three items in the catalog or the serials holding list.

Shelf check -- explain to patrons that we do not have the staff to check shelves but, staff may check the status of a title in UR Online.

Personal calls should not be made at desk. Calls to vendors, publishers, etc. should not be made at the desk either unless directly related to reference desk service.

Patron use of the telephone is not allowed unless they need to check the availability of a book at a local library or if they are in an emergency situation. There are public telephones and campus phones on B-1 behind the stairs.

In transferring a patron to another department, wait until a person answers.

E.   OPENING AND CLOSING THE REFERENCE DESK

OPENING THE REFERENCE DESK:

The staff member scheduled at the Reference Desk should arrive a few minutes earlier so that reference services can be initiated at the time the desk opens.

1. The telephone should be installed at the desk and checked for messages on Audix.
2. Unlock the two reference desk file drawers.
3. OCLC and all CD-ROM equipment should be turned on and appropriate disks should be loaded.
4. Position reference sign to "OPEN".
5. A new statistic form should be ready if needed. The desk should be clean and all ready reference materials should be shelved.

At closing time, librarians are responsible for the following:

1. Inspect the reference desk area and do any reshelving and general cleanup as needed.
2. Turn off all CD-ROM equipment except InfroTrac and Newsbank.
3. Check messages on Audix. Unplug reference telephone and place in reference office.
4. Position sign to indicate the Reference Desk is closed.
5. Lock the two reference desk drawers and put keys in reference office filing cabinet. Lock the reference office, making sure computer is off, lights are off and Dynix screen is blank.

F.   STAFFING AND SCHEDULING

During regular semester hours, the desk is staffed from 9:00 a.m. - 10:00 p.m., Monday through Thursday; 9:00 a.m. - 5:00 p.m. on Friday; 1:00 p.m. - 5:00 p.m. on Saturday and 1:00 p.m. - 10:00 p.m. on Sunday.

When a reference staff member is scheduled for back-up hours, it is expected that they will be readily available in the reference office or reference room so that the person on duty may call for needed assistance.

Calling in Sick

When calling in sick, notify the Director of Public Services. In her absence, notify the library secretary or reference colleagues.

Desk Work

It is important to be as approachable as possible while on the desk. When desk traffic is slow, however, staff may work on projects that don't require too much concentration or table space. Reviewing the Reading File and new reference books are excellent desk projects when business is slow.

Changes in scheduled desk hours

Reference staff should ask their back-up to trade or cover hours first. If that is impossible they should ask another librarian to trade hours. All changes should be given to the Coordinator of Reference Services and noted on the departmental calendar.

G. READY REFERENCE LOANS

High-use reference materials are kept behind the desk and are only to be used on a temporary basis in the library, preferably in the reference area. Users are asked to sign the pink cards, record their name and ID number and return the item to the reference desk within 2 hours.

H. REFERENCE COLLECTION CIRCULATION

In general, reference books do not circulate. Use careful discretion in allowing reference materials to circulate. Question the patron carefully and try to find a circulating item for him/her if at all possible. Check with the appropriate liaison librarian to determine if it could be a high-use item. A reference book may circulate if approved by the Reference librarian on duty or in consultation with the Coordinator of Reference Services. Reference staff must accompany the user to the Circulation Desk or write a note giving permission for the user to check out the Reference material.

I. REPORTING PROBLEMS OR COMPLAINTS

Problem Patrons

Report to Director of Public Services or Night Supervisor as the situation requires. If none of the above are available, call campus police.

Building Problems

Report to the Director of Public Services or the Night Supervisor.

In Case of Fire/Injury/Emergency

Call campus police and/or inform the Director of Public Services or the Night Supervisor.

Library Police Questions or Complaints

Do not argue with the patron, simply refer them in a polite manner to the appropriate department or division head once you have notified a specific person that the patron is being sent to him or her. Report all complaints to the Director of Public Services.

J. SPECIAL INQUIRIES

Class Assignments

If there is an entire class asking the same questions, leave word in the class assignment file at the reference desk and make a note for colleagues to read it.

Legal and Medical Advice

Information of this nature should never be interpreted to the patron. The best situation is to direct the patron to proper medical or legal sources where they can find their own answers. Always remind the patron that you are not qualified to give such advice.

City Directory Information

No more than three items in the city directory will be checked for a telephone patron. If more information is needed, they are invited to come to Boatwright and use the source. Patrons must give specific name, address or phone number to be checked.

Compositional/Writing Questions

Students are encouraged to contact the UR Writing Lab. Reference staff should refrain from offering advice on writing and composition. Proofreading is not provided by either the Reference or the Writing Center staff since this constitutes an Honor Code violation.

Interlibrary Loan

See Interlibrary Loan section in Public Service Handbook.

Library Tours/Classes

Refer requests as follows:
> University group tours to Marcia Whitehead;
> High School or other non-University groups to Lucretia McCulley.

Business Reference Questions

Refer to the staff of the Business Information Center.

UNIVERSITY OF RICHMOND LIBRARIES REFERENCE SERVICE
General Reference Department Service

The Reference Department has been making some changes to the traditional pattern of reference service, with the goal of improving the quality of our service to our patrons. We have followed with interest the ongoing discussion within the profession about departures from adherence to the idea that the reference desk is **the** point of service for reference needs, and have devised a multi-layered approach to service.

HOURS AND STAFFING

During the 95/96 academic year the reference desk will be open from 10 am until 10 pm Monday through Thursday, from 10 am to 5 pm on Friday, 1 - 5 pm on Saturday and 1 - 10 pm on Sunday. Reference librarians are scheduled to work at the desk each weekday from 11-3, each evening from 6-10, and Sunday from 1-10. The reference associate works at the desk from 10-11 and from 3-5 each week day. Trained students staff the desk from 5-6 Monday through Thursday, and 1-5 on Friday and Saturday. Reference librarians are scheduled to be "on call" during the times the desk is staffed by students.

LEVELS OF SERVICE

Reference Desk   The reference desk remains the usual first point of contact. Directional and ready reference questions are handled here and referrals to other levels of service are frequently arranged at this point.
Roving   Everyone working at the reference desk is encouraged to take a proactive approach to service and roam through the area to offer assistance, rather than only being reactive and remaining at the desk.
Appointments   All of the reference librarians are available for appointments if someone needs more help than can be provided as part of regular desk service. An appointment book is maintained at the desk in which each librarian blocks out time for appointments. Anyone working at the desk can make an appointment for the patron with a librarian, and choose the appropriate subject specialist if needed.
Research Consultations   If more in depth help is needed with an assignment, a student can request a consultation by filling out the appropriate form. The librarian whose subject specialties most nearly match the needs of the student will contact the student and arrange for the consultation.

We will be adding an new point of contact for the first time this year. From the UR Libraries' Homepage a patron can choose the General Reference Web Page and find sources of information for which we have provided links to other locations on the Internet. Patrons can also send reference questions to the Reference Desk e-mail address.

ORIENTATION MANUAL

for the new

REFERENCE LIBRARIAN

Reference Department
July 1983
  Revised September 1994

INTRODUCTION

Reference Librarians are the most visible and accessible of all WPC Librarians. In order for them to facilitate access to the Library's collection or to refer users to sources of information, they must know the full range of services and resources available.

This orientation manual will provide the outline necessary to acquaint the new staff member with the operation of the library as a whole, and the role of the Reference Department within the organization. The following provides only the framework, and it is the responsibility of a new reference librarian to fill in the relevant information by visiting each Department and becoming familiar with those areas outlined.

GOALS OF REFERENCE SERVICE

The primary purpose of the Reference Department is to facilitate access to the Library's collections through direct personal services to the Library's users and to support the College's instructional program by providing formal and informal library instruction.

Specifically, the goals of the Reference Department are threefold

1) to educate patrons in the use of the library,
2) to assist patrons in finding information,
3) to teach patrons to think critically about the
   use of information resources

While recognizing that a number of patron variables such as readiness, interest, understanding of the assignment or the information need and perseverance as well as time, activity level at the reference desk, librarian knowledge/understanding of the question and interpersonal factors, can interfere with the education/service mix, our goal remains to pursue the highest level of education and service possible with each reference transaction.

PHILOSOPHICAL APPROACH TO REFERENCE SERVICE

Apart from "ready reference" types of inquiries, assistance to users will generally take the form of providing the information itself. This guidance however should not be forced and it is the responsibility of the reference librarian to use judgement in determining what type of assistance best serves the needs of the patron.

The individual reference librarian should assume an active service posture and must exercise judgement in determining the needs of the user in specific situations and the amount of time available. The librarian should take a reasonable amount of time to conduct a reference interview and should make an effort to ascertain whether or not the assistance provided met the patron's needs. In addition, the librarian should provide referrals to other departments, libraries and organizations as appropriate.

SERVICE POLICIES

The following policies should provide general guidelines for service. The reference librarian is expected to exercise independent judgement in meeting the information needs of the patrons.

1.   All patrons should be assisted on a first-come, first-served basis. The reference librarian should ascertain in any individuals waiting in line have simple questions that can be answered quickly before engaging in a lengthy transaction. Patrons waiting in line should be acknowledge verbally or non-verbally so that they are aware that you intend to provide assistance.

There is no distinction made based on who a patron is. If there is an emergency call from the President's office, it should be handled as promptly as possible.

2.   Reference librarians answer queries by phone, letter and email in addition to providing in person assistance. If there is heavy activity at the reference desk, it is preferable to take the essential information from a telephone caller and return the call as quickly as possible.

3.   Assistance should be offered at the reference desk or at the point of use. If it is necessary to leave the reference area, back-up assistance should be arranged if possible. If the reference librarian is working alone, it is the responsibility of the librarian to minimize time away from the desk, or to periodically check back to make sure that others are not waiting. The reference librarian should answer the phone.

4.   For difficult questions or lengthy instruction, it is appropriate the make a separate appointment with the patron during a time when the librarian is not scheduled at the reference desk.

5.   Reference librarians should not give medical, business, or legal advice. It is appropriate to read a selection from a text. The source should be cited.

6.   Reference librarians and staff work as a team. It is appropriate to share information with colleagues and to help a colleague who is providing information to a patron. Any interruption of a colleague should be done discreetly.

7.   The librarian on duty should make a reasonable effort to answer a question before referral to a colleague.

8.   An online search may be performed at the reference desk if time allows. Quick searches ("queries") may be performed at no charge if the expected result is only a few hits and inexpensive. Extensive searches are conducted on a fee-basis and should be referred to the primary searcher or completed when not at the desk.

9.   If the desk is understaffed, the reference librarian should contact others in the reference office who may be available to help out.

GENERAL POLICIES AND SERVICE OF THE REFERENCE DEPARTMENT

To be reviewed with the Head of Reference unless otherwise noted.

A.   Policies
See Library Policy Manual for library-wide and other departmental policies

    1.   Circulation of reference, documents, vertical file
    2.   ILL policies and procedures (see Marie Monteagudo)
    3.   Database searching (see Bill Duffy)
    4.   Use of Other Collections
            Reciprocal borrowing
            Faculty handout
            Princeton Access Card
            Letters of reference
            Telephone assistance
    5.   Documents
    6.   Favors for faculty
            Extensive research
            Copying
    7.   Missing books/vandalism
            Shelf check
            Missing reference book form
            Reporting vandalism
            ILL for missing pages
    8.   Scheduling
            Calendars
             Vacations
             Comp days
             Medical Days
    9.   Ordering reference materials
    10.   Requests for instruction
    11.   Guidelines for Absence
    12.   Typing Assistance
    13.   Students Assistants
    14.   Relationship with ERC
    15.   Archives & "Archival" type material
    16.   Special Collections
    17.   N.J. Collection
    18.   Keys

B.   Arrangement and location of collection

    1.   Reference stacks - folio
    2.   N.J. Documents

3.   Special Tables
        Business
        News
        Media
        Grants
        Statistics
4.   Encyclopedia, atlases
5.   Index tables
6.   Index stacks
7.   ERIC microfiche
8.   Reference Microforms
9.   Storage
10.   Ready Reference
11.   Masters Theses
12.   Paterson Papers
13.   Vertical File
14.   JFK Materials
15.   Telephone directories
16.   Reserves
        Comprehensive exams

C.   Orientations

1.   PAC
2.   OCLC
3.   VAC NOTES, Email
4.   Law Collection
5.   Health Collection
6.   Business Collection
7.   Other

D.   Electronic Reference Center (Fran Novick)

E.   Periodical and Microform Collection (Jackie Hill

1.   Location
2.   Contents of collection
3.   Use of guides to the collection

F.   Curriculum Materials (Marie Radford)

1.   Location
2.   Contents and purpose of the collection
3.   Arrangement
4.   Special materials (KCDL, Curriculum guides)
5.   Services

6.   Microcomputer and software collection
7.   Reference assistance
8.   Bibliographies

G.   AV Department (Jane Hutchison)

1.   Location
2.   Nature of collection
3.   Access to collection
4.   Services offered
5.   Reference assistance

H.   Special Collections (Robert Wolk)

1.   Contents and arrangement
2.   Services offered
3.   How to Access materials
4.   Non-circulation policy

I.   Technical Services (Amy Job)

1.   PAC
2.   Shelflist
3.   Overview of cataloging procedures

J.   Archives

1.   Location
2.   Nature of collection
3.   Services and policies in regard to access

K.   Library Instruction (Robert Wolk)

1.   Formal Instruction procedures
2.   Freshmen Orientation
3.   Instructional Handouts
4.   Transparencies
5.   Instruction Room

L.   Collection Development (Anne Ciliberti)

1.   Role of Selector
2.   Function of O & R
3.   Collection Development Policy
4.   Overview of O & R Procedures

M.   Automation (Maureen Riley)

N.   Lending Services/Reserve (Yvonne Roux)

O.   Miscellaneous Services & Information

      1.   Tattle-tape
      2.   Emergency procedures
      3.   Photocopiers
      4.   Change machines
      5.   Vendacard
      6.   Calendar
      7.   Food/smoking
      8.   Suggestion box
      9.   Supplies